sixties design

design

Philippe Garner

TASCHEN

KÖLN LONDON LOS ANGELES MADRID PARIS TOKYO

FRONT COVER
Verner and Marianne Panton's home in Basle-Binningen, 1973 –
showing *Ring Lights* designed for Louis Poulsen in 1969
© 2003 Panton Archiv, Basle

BACK COVER
Poul Volther, *Model no. EJ 605 Corona* chair for Erik Jørgensen,
1961
© 2003 Courtesy Bonhams & Butterfields

PAGE 2/3
Still from the film "Gimme Shelter", documenting the Rolling
Stones' Altamont concert, December 1969

PAGE 6/7
Robert Rauschenberg: "Axle", oil and silk screen print on canvas,
four panels, 1964

© 2003 TASCHEN GmbH
Hohenzollernring 53, D-50672 Köln
www.taschen.com

Original edition: © 1996 Benedikt Taschen Verlag GmbH
© 1996 for the text: Philippe Garner, London
© 2003 VG Bild-Kunst, Bonn for the works by Blake, Hamilton,
Lichtenstein, Rauschenberg, Stella, Vasarely and Wesselmann

Designed by Angelika Muthesius, Cologne
German translation by Thomas Berg, Bonn, and
Bettina Blumenberg, Munich (chapter 3)
French translation by Frédérique Daber, Cahors

Printed in Italy
ISBN 3-8228-2937-4

Contents | Inhalt | Sommaire

In January 1967 the Italian magazine *Domus* published a series of snapshots by Ettore Sottsass Jr. In a feature entitled "Memoires di panna montata" ("Whipped cream memoirs") he presented the results of a visual note-taking in London the previous October. Sottsass was fascinated by the atmosphere and specifically the graphics of London's popular culture. He had photographed the boutiques, their interiors, window displays and signs, the graffiti, the painted or neon visual language of a vibrant counter-culture. Amidst such logos as "Pacesetters", "Palisades" and "Male West One", he found a new world which had turned its back on "the little black dress and the string of cultured pearls, and had also finished with the Swiss-Dutch approach". Sottsass had identified the signals of the defining *Zeitgeist* of the Sixties.

The following year, 1968, saw the completion of Mies van der Rohe's last great project, his National Gallery building in Berlin. This project distilled the sublime essence of the Mies philosophy. It was composed on a cube grid, much of which was underground. The visible façades were minimalist compositions – walls of glass contained within a finely disciplined frame of strict horizontals and verticals. Mies gave Germany a monument to the International Style. His brand of purism had its origins in his Bauhaus years, but had lost sight of the school's founding ideals. The original utopianism of the Bauhaus had been eroded by the temptations of corporate America. The International Style emerged as the post-war torch-bearer of the Modern Movement but in a new guise, with the emphasis on formal values, and by the early Sixties was a crucial influence in all areas of design.

Sottsass observed the triumph of the consumer, particularly the young consumer, the idea of style and design imposing themselves from the street up. Mies van der Rohe defined an autocratic role for the designer. His brand of International Modernism spoke of power, refinement and elitism. Between the rich explosion of popular culture, filled with symbol and metaphor, and the idea of design as a process of refinement towards the Platonic ideal of perfect form, lies the fecund and fascinating story of style and design in the Sixties.

Numerous cross-currents and influences contributed to make the decade so fertile a period of creative activity within a prevailing culture of plenty, a culture of optimism and possibility. Design in the Sixties can be identified as central to the processes of consumerism and communication. Design helped define groups and therefore markets. Style and design gave form to collective moods and needs and translated those needs into materialistic ambitions. Design played a key role in the momentum of the market place, and the greatest achievements in style and design tended inevitably to be associated with nations enjoying the fruits of growth economies. The international story of style and design was largely predicated around the axis of the American

Im Januar 1967 veröffentlichte die italienische Zeitschrift »Domus« eine Reihe von Schnappschüssen von Ettore Sottsass Jr. Unter der Überschrift »Memoires di panna montata« (»Schlagsahne-Memoiren«) stellte Sottsass im begleitenden Artikel seine fotografischen Notizen vor, die er bei einem Streifzug durch London im Oktober des vorangegangenen Jahres aufgenommen hatte. Sottsass hatten die Atmosphäre und insbesondere die sichtbaren Zeichen der Londoner Alltagskultur fasziniert. Seine Fotografien zeigten die Modeboutiquen mit ihren Einrichtungen, Schaufensterdekorationen und Reklametafeln. Sie zeigten aber auch gemaltes oder durch Neonlicht gestaltetes Graffiti, den visualisierten Ausdruck einer vibrierenden Gegenkultur. Inmitten von Logos wie »Pacesetters«, »Palisades« oder »Male West One« hatte er eine neue Welt entdeckt, die dem »kleinen Schwarzen« und der »Perlenkette« den Rücken zugekehrt und die sich ebenfalls von dem, was er den »schweizerisch-niederländischen Ansatz« nannte, losgesagt hatte. Sottsass hatte die charakteristischen Signale des Zeitgeistes der sechziger Jahre erkannt.

Im Jahr darauf, 1968, wurde mit der Neuen Nationalgalerie in Berlin das letzte große Bauprojekt Mies van der Rohes fertiggestellt – ein Gebäude, das die Philosophie seines Erbauers in höchster Vollendung verkörpert. Der zum größten Teil unterirdische Bau basiert auf einer kubischen Grundstruktur. Die sichtbare Glasfassade ist durch die elegant gegliederte Rahmung aus strengen Horizontalen und Vertikalen wie eine minimalistische Komposition angelegt. Mies van der Rohe schuf mit diesem Bau ein Denkmal des Internationalen Stils in Deutschland. Sein puristischer Baustil ging zwar auf seine Zeit am Bauhaus zurück, ließ jedoch erkennen, daß er die Gründungsideale dieser Schule inzwischen aus den Augen verloren hatte. Die Utopien des Bauhauses waren den Versuchungen des kapitalistischen Amerikas scheinbar nicht gewachsen gewesen. Der Internationale Stil fungierte in den Nachkriegsjahren als Schrittmacher der Moderne mit einem neuen Erscheinungsbild: Der Schwerpunkt lag jetzt auf formalen Werten. Anfang der sechziger Jahre übte der Internationale Stil Einfluß auf alle Bereiche der Gestaltung aus.

Sottsass beobachtete den Erfolg bei den Konsumenten, insbesondere bei den jüngeren, und erkannte, daß deren Vorstellungen von zeitgemäßem Stil und Design von den vielfältigen Einflüssen des Alltags bestimmt wurden. Mies van der Rohe sah den Designer dagegen in einer autokratischen Rolle. Sein Beitrag zur Internationalen Moderne stand stellvertretend für Macht, Kultiviertheit und Elitebewußtsein. Die Stil- und Designgeschichte der sechziger Jahren wurde also von zwei verschiedenen Polen bestimmt: einerseits von dem gewaltigen Ausbruch einer Alltagskultur voller Symbole und Metaphern und zum anderen von dem Glauben an ein Design, an dessen Ende das platonische Ideal der vollkommenen Form stehen sollte.

1

Prologue

Prolog

Prologue

En janvier 1967, le magazine italien «Domus» publia une série de clichés d'Ettore Sottsass Jr. qui, dans un reportage intitulé «Memoires di panna montata» («Mémoires à la Chantilly»), présentait des photos prises à Londres au cours de l'automne précédent. Fasciné par l'atmosphère, et surtout par les manifestations graphiques, de la culture populaire londonienne, il avait photographié les boutiques, extérieurs et intérieurs, les vitrines et les enseignes, les graffiti, tout le langage visuel, à la peinture ou au néon, d'une vibrante contre-culture. Un monde nouveau, illustré par des noms comme «Pacesetters», «Palisades» et «Male West One», se révélait à lui, un monde qui tournait le dos «à la petite robe noire et au collier de perles, et qui en avait fini avec la culture suisso-hollandaise». Ce que Sottsass avait capté là, c'était l'esprit des années soixante.

L'année suivante, 1968, vit l'achèvement du dernier grand projet de Mies van der Rohe, son Musée national de Berlin, pur symbole de la philosophie de l'architecte. Il se composait d'un cube dont la majeure partie était souterraine. Les façades apparentes étaient des compositions minimalistes faites de strictes lignes horizontales et verticales. Avec cette œuvre, Mies dotait l'Allemagne d'un fleuron du Style International. Le purisme qui était celui de ce créateur avait ses racines dans ses années au sein du Bauhaus mais il s'était, au fil du temps, éloigné des doctrines de cette école. L'utopisme originel s'était émoussé sous l'effet des tentations de l'Amérique du monde des affaires. Le Style International se fit, après la guerre, le champion du modernisme mais sous une forme différente, dans laquelle l'accent était mis sur les valeurs formelles. Au début des années soixante, son influence était prédominant dans tous les domaines du design.

Ce que décrit Sottsass c'est le triomphe du consommateur, en particulier du jeune consommateur, et le phénomène selon lequel style et design s'imposent depuis la rue. Pour Mies van der Rohe, par contre, le designer est un autocrate. Son idée du Modernisme international respire la puissance, le raffinement et l'élitisme. C'est entre la fabuleuse explosion de la culture populaire, pétrie de symboles et de métaphores, et la conception du design porteur de l'idéal platonicien de la forme parfaite que s'est formée la riche et passionnante histoire du style et du design des années soixante.

Nombreux sont les courants et les influences qui ont contribué à faire de cette décennie une période d'intense créativité au sein d'un climat général d'abondance, d'optimisme et d'opportunités nouvelles. Le design des années soixante a la particularité de jouer un rôle central dans les processus de consommation et de communication. En contribuant à définir les groupes sociologiques, il définit aussi les marchés. Ces deux éléments, style et design, ont donné des formes à des attitudes collectives, des besoins qui se sont traduits par un désir matérialiste de possession. Etant donné son rôle-clé dans l'élan éco-

Portrait of Ettore Sottsass Jr.

PAGE 11 TOP
AND PAGES 12/13
"Domus" magazine, January
1967, "Memoires di panna
montata", by Ettore Sottsass
Jr.

PAGE 11 BOTTOM
Nationalgalerie Berlin,
designed by **Ludwig Mies van
der Rohe**, 1968

economy, the rebuilt and flourishing economies of Japan and West Germany, Great Britain, Italy, the Scandinavian countries and France.

The United States established a template for the culture of consumerism with its attendant design functions. Evolutionary product design and styling, brand and corporate imaging, marketing and advertising were defined and refined. In Germany and Japan, native skills were harnessed to the processes of rebuilding economic strength and influence. Discipline, methodology and technological resources were applied to emerging markets with particular success in the manufacture of automobiles and electrical and electronic goods. Britain was enjoying the turn-around from post-war austerity, adjusting from its traditions as a manufacturing nation to a new role dominated by service and high-skilled technological industries. The new Britain was galvanised by Harold Wilson's vision, defined in 1963, of change, technology, automation and scientific revolution. Italy, meanwhile, was enjoying its own *rinascenza* in the industrial cities of the north, and the intimate linking of the design and manufacturing processes were to give Italy an unprecedented international influence which flourishes to this day.

Commercial television, the various other advertising media, consumer magazines and city sign systems, both commercial and practical, emerged as challenging and exciting new disciplines in the interface between consumer and product, promising, seducing, fuelling and directing. The role of design extended way beyond the need for harmony between form and function. The designer became a communicator, giving form to products not in the abstract but within a culture, for a market place. Fashion played its part and the language of design was obliged to devise a constantly evolving vernacular derived both from popular culture and from the fine arts. Never before had there been so fruitful a dialogue between the so-called "fine" and "commercial" arts. Writing in 1972 in their introduction to the study *Art without Boundaries: 1950–70*, authors Gerald Woods, Philip Thompson and John Williams noted that "At one time it was easy to distinguish between the 'fine' artist and the commercial artist. It is now less easy. The qualities which differentiated the one from the other are now often common to both ... During the last twenty years or so, barriers have been broken down; and they are still being broken down."

Consumer products, advertising and the popular media had fascinated a significant number of artists since the Fifties. Through the Sixties, ideas on colour, contrast, pattern and motif were liberally exchanged between artists working in every discipline. Pop Art and Pop culture established a dialogue. Every new "ism" in art found its corollary in fashion and design. "Op", "Kinetic", "Hard Edge" and other experiments were rapidly integrated into the widest culture.

Zahlreiche Gegenströmungen und Einflüsse sorgten dafür, daß die sechziger Jahre – die durch Überfluß und Optimismus geprägt waren – zu einer äußerst kreativen Periode wurden. Dem Design kam in bezug auf das Konsum- und Kommunikationsverhalten eine entscheidende Bedeutung zu. Mit Hilfe von Design ließen sich Zielgruppen ausmachen und somit Märkte erschließen. Stil und Design beeinflußten die Stimmungen und die Bedürfnisse der Massen, was sich unmittelbar auf die materiellen Wünsche auswirkte. Design war damit für das Wirtschaftswachstum von entscheidender Bedeutung. Es ist deshalb nicht verwunderlich, daß die größten Leistungen auf dem Gebiet von Stil und Design bald eine nationale Bedeutung gewann, vor allem in Ländern mit einer aufstrebenden Wirtschaft. Die Geschichte des Internationalen Stils und des Designs vollzog sich größtenteils im Bereich der amerikanischen Wirtschaft, der wiederauferstandenen und florierenden Ökonomien Japans, Westdeutschlands, Englands, Italiens, der skandinavischen Länder und Frankreichs.

Was das Konsumverhalten betrifft und die eng damit verbundenen Zielsetzungen des Designs, übernahmen die USA eine Vorreiterrolle. Die Entwicklung und Gestaltung von Produkten, die Imagebildung von Markenzeichen und Unternehmen, das Marketing sowie die Reklame wurden hier definiert und ständig verbessert. In Deutschland und Japan besann man sich dagegen auf ursprüngliche Fertigkeiten, um wieder an wirtschaftlicher Stärke und Einfluß zu gewinnen. Disziplin, Methodik und technologische Ressourcen wurden in den Dienst neuer Märkte gestellt, was sich besonders in der Automobil- und Elektroindustrie erfolgreich bemerkbar machte. England erlebte nach den Einschränkungen der Nachkriegszeit eine Trendwende. Angespornt durch die von Harold Wilson 1963 fomulierte Vision »eines Wandels, einer Revolution der Technologie, der Automation und der Wissenschaften«, paßte sich das Land dem neuen Bedarf an Dienstleistungsunternehmen und hochspezialisierten technologischen Industrien an. Unterdessen erfuhren die nördlichen Industriestädte Italiens ihre eigene »rinascenza« (Wiedergeburt). Die engen Bindungen zwischen Design und Herstellungsprozessen gaben Italien einen internationalen Einfluß, der bis heute anhält.

Das Werbefernsehen und andere Reklamemedien, Verbraucherzeitschriften und die sowohl für kommerzielle als auch für praktische Zwecke benötigten Systeme der Stadtbeschilderung erschlossen den Designern abwechslungsreiche und interessante neue Aufgabenbereiche. Die Arbeit an der Schnittstelle zwischen Verbraucher und Produkt erwies sich als vielversprechend, verführerisch, herausfordernd und richtungsweisend. Die Aufgabe des Designs ging weit über die bloße Harmonisierung von Form und Funktion hinaus. Der Designer übernahm die Rolle eines Vermittlers. Er gestaltete Produkte nun nicht mehr nach rein formalen Kriterien, sondern für den

nomique, on comprend que ce soit dans les pays à forte croissance économique que le design a produit ses fruits les plus remarquables. Son histoire se fait donc surtout autour de l'économie américaine et de celles, reconstruites et désormais florissantes, du Japon, de l'Allemagne de l'Ouest, de la Grande-Bretagne, de l'Italie, des pays scandinaves et de la France.

En matière de culture de consommation, les Etats-Unis sont le point de référence. C'est là que furent définies et que s'affinèrent les règles du design industriel, de la fabrication d'une «image de marque» des produits et des entreprises, du marketing et de la publicité. En Allemagne et au Japon, on s'attelait à la reconstruction économique en tirant parti des compétences nationales. C'est dans le domaine de la production automobile et dans celui de l'appareillage électrique et électronique que cette recette, faite de discipline, de méthodologie et de ressources technologiques, connut le plus de succès. La Grande-Bretagne avait passé le cap de l'austérité de l'après-guerre et, tournant le dos à ses traditions industrielles, devenait un pays de services et de technologies hyper-spécialisées. Le pays s'était totalement impliqué à réaliser le programme décrit par Harold Wilson en 1963: changement, technologie, automatisation et révolution scientifique. A la même époque, l'Italie connaissait, dans ses cités industrielles du nord, son propre «rinascenza» (renouveau). La rencontre du design et de nouveaux processus de fabrication allait donner au pays une avance importante dans ce domaine, avance qu'il a conservée jusqu'à nos jours.

La télévision commerciale et les divers médias publicitaires, la presse de consommation et les systèmes d'affichage, que leur rôle soit commercial ou pratique, devenaient de nouvelles et exaltantes disciplines qui établissaient entre consommateur et produit de consommation, un langage tout de promesses, de séduction, d'encouragement et de conseil. Le design n'était plus seulement là pour créer une harmonie entre forme et fonction, il était devenu un moyen de communication; il donnait forme à des produits, non pas dans l'abstrait mais au sein d'une culture, pour un marché donné. La mode intervenant aussi, le design dut mettre au point un jargon en évolution perpétuelle, inspiré à la fois de la culture populaire et des beaux-arts. On n'avait jamais assisté à un dialogue aussi riche entre l'art dit «noble» et l'art «commercial». Dans l'introduction à leur étude parue en 1972 «Art without Boundaries: 1950–70», Gerald Woods, Philip Thompson et John Williams notent: «Il fut un temps où il était facile de faire la distinction entre un artiste avec un grand A et un artiste commercial. Cette époque est révolue. Les particularités qui les distinguaient leur sont maintenant souvent communes … Au cours des vingt dernières années, on s'est mis à renverser des barrières et on n'a pas fini de le faire.» Depuis les années cinquante, un grand nombre d'artistes s'était enthousiasmé pour la production de

NO

TO WALTON STREET
DIVERSION

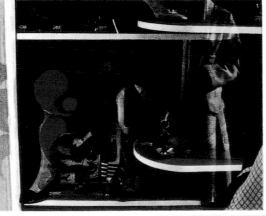

PACESETTERS

MALE
WEST
ONE

W. 1.

The mood of possibility was symbolically defined in the promise made in 1962 by the incumbent young President Kennedy that American astronauts would walk on the moon before the close of the decade. Science fiction seemed determined to become science fact and technological progress offered prospects of greatly enhanced life styles. Global resources still seemed infinite, as did man's ability to visualise and then create a better environment. The decade was buoyed by the dream of a space age which took its cue from the NASA programme and which created an iconography of futuristic fashions, artifacts and environments. Dazzling silver and white spaces were the *tabula rasa* on which visionary designers turned an idea of tomorrow into a tangible though symbolic today.

The idea of at last being able to create a brave new world exploiting accelerated technological advance brought sharply into focus the disciplines of town planning and urban regeneration. Theories first articulated some thirty or forty years earlier by Le Corbusier and contemporary utopians were now to be put to the test, with varying degrees of success. Certain grandiose schemes such as the ambitious Brasilia project, which was completed at the beginning of the decade, were eventually acknowledged as working better on the drawing board than in practice. Urban dreams were seldom translated into satisfactory realities. The decade inspired some fine, isolated examples of architecture, though the problems of meeting housing needs in cities with burgeoning populations, of accommodating more and more cars into old city centres and of devising city schemes to cope with changing patterns of life, were recognised but rarely resolved. The prevailing optimism of the early Sixties and the subsequent mood of disillusion were challenged by radical debate in architecture and urban planning. The provocative theories and projects of such groups as Archigram in Great Britain, or Archizoom and Superstudio in Italy, took the subject into quite new terrain.

By the close of the decade a polarisation of the design debate had become more clearly evident. The idea of good taste, of a Modernist perfection of form, was derided by the increasingly vocal "Anti-Design" lobby, which sought rather to explore the metaphors and complexities of the language of design. This conflict came to a head in the 1968 Milan Triennale, which was shut down by protestors. It was a conflict of ambitions between the classicists and the iconoclasts, though the story of Sixties design is often a reminder that these opposites can not only co-exist but that, indeed, each needs the other as a foil.

Such, then, are some of the strands which this essay will explore. It is not possible to be encyclopaedic within the context of so brief a survey and the author must beg the reader's indulgence for many omissions and for too brief references to so many talents, each worthy of very

Absatzmarkt einer bestimmten Kultur. Der modische Wandel spielte ebenfalls eine wichtige Rolle. Deshalb mußte eine Formensprache erarbeitet werden, die anpaßbar war und die sich sowohl an der Alltagskultur als auch an den bildenden Künsten orientierte. In ihrem Vorwort zu der Publikation »Art without Boundaries: 1950–70« stellten Gerald Woods, Philip Thompson und John Williams 1972 fest, daß »es im Gegensatz zu heute früher einfacher war, den ›bildenden‹ vom ›angewandten‹ Künstler zu unterscheiden. Die Qualitäten, die den einen von dem anderen unterschieden, sind heutzutage häufig beiden gemein«. Konsumwaren und Massenmedien übten seit den fünfziger Jahren einen starken Einfluß auf viele Künstler aus. Seit den sechziger Jahren fand zwischen Künstlern aller Disziplinen ein freimütiger Austausch von Farb-, Kontrast-, Muster- und Motivideen statt. Pop Art und Pop-Kultur inspirierten sich gegenseitig. Jeder neue »Ismus« in der Kunst fand sein Pendant in der Mode und im Design. »Op«, »Kinetic«, »Hard Edge« und andere künstlerische Experimente wurden sofort in die Gesamtkultur integriert.

Das Gefühl unbegrenzter Möglichkeiten fand seinen symbolischen Ausdruck, als Präsident Kennedy 1962 versprach, daß amerikanische Astronauten noch vor Ende des Jahrzehnts den Mond betreten würden. Sciencefiction war auf dem besten Wege, Wirklichkeit zu werden. Der technologische Fortschritt hob den Lebensstandard. Die globalen Ressourcen schienen immer noch genauso unerschöpflich zu sein wie die Fähigkeit der Menschheit, eine besser ausgestattete Umgebung zu planen und zu erschaffen. Der von der NASA angeregte Traum vom Raumfahrt-Zeitalter beflügelte die Phantasie der sechziger Jahre und führte in der Mode, in der Kunst und der Innenarchitektur zu einem futuristischen Stil. Weiße, silbern schimmernde Räume bildeten die »tabula rasa«, auf der visionäre Designer ihre Zukunftsphantasien in die Symbolik der Gegenwart umsetzten.

Die Überzeugung, daß mit Hilfe des rasanten technologischen Fortschritts endlich eine ideale Welt errichtet werden könne, rückte Städteplanung und Stadterneuerung in den Mittelpunkt des Interesses. Städtebauliche Theorien, die von Le Corbusier und anderen Utopisten schon vor dreißig bis vierzig Jahren formuliert worden waren, wurden nun in die Wirklichkeit umgesetzt. Am Ende blieb jedoch die Erkenntnis, daß einige der bombastischen Vorhaben, wie etwa das ehrgeizige, gegen Ende der sechziger Jahre fertiggestellte Brasilia-Projekt, auf dem Zeichenbrett besser funktionierten als in der Wirklichkeit. In den sechziger Jahren entstanden zwar vereinzelt anspruchsvolle Architekturen; es ergaben sich aber durch den wachsenden Wohnbedarf in den Städten mit steigender Bevölkerungszahl, durch den zunehmenden Verkehr in den alten Stadtkernen und durch die Entwicklung von Bebauungsplänen, die den veränderten Lebensformen gerecht werden sollten, Probleme, die nur selten gelöst wurden, obwohl man sie durchaus erkannte. Der

consommation et les médias populaires. Tout au long
des années soixante, il y eut un brassage d'idées inter-
disciplinaires sur les thèmes de la couleur, du contraste,
de la forme et du motif. Un dialogue s'établit entre le
pop art et la culture Pop. Toute nouvelle école artistique
eut son corollaire dans les domaines de la mode et du
design. Des expérimentations comme l'op art ou l'art
kinétique furent rapidement assimilées par le climat cul-
turel général.

Cette idée ambiante que tout était possible se résume
de façon symbolique dans l'engagement de Kennedy,
nouveau jeune président des Etats-Unis: des astronautes
américains marcheraient sur la lune avant la fin de la
décennie. La fiction semblait vouloir devenir réalité et
l'avance technologique faisait entrevoir des progrès
fabuleux. Les ressources planétaires paraissaient encore
inépuisables, comme d'ailleurs la capacité des êtres
humains à imaginer, puis à créer, un environnement
meilleur. Toute la décennie était portée par le rêve spatial, basé sur les programmes de la NASA qui générèrent
une iconographie futuriste touchant la mode, les objets
et la décoration. Des espaces éblouissants, blancs et
argent, fournirent aux designers la «tabula rasa» néces-
saire pour créer à partir d'une idée de l'avenir un présent
à la fois tangible et symbolique.

L'idée que, grâce à l'accélération technologique, se
profilait enfin le meilleur des mondes mit l'urbanisation
et la réhabilitation architecturale sous le feu des projec-
teurs. Des théories énoncées trente ou quarante ans
plus tôt par Le Corbusier et autres utopistes de l'époque
allaient être mises en pratique avec plus ou moins de
succès. On dut bien constater que certains projets grandioses, comme celui de Brasília qui fut achevé au début
de la décennie, étaient plus satisfaisants sur le papier
que dans la réalité. Il n'y eut que peu de réussites dans
le domaine de l'urbanisme. Il y eut quelques belles réalisations architecturales isolées mais si les problèmes
du logement pour la population croissante des villes, de
la circulation de plus en plus dense dans les quartiers
anciens et de l'adaptation aux mœurs urbaines nouvelles, furent bel et bien reconnus, ils ne furent que rare-
ment résolus. L'optimisme prévalant du début des
années soixante et les désillusions qui s'ensuivirent se
trouvèrent confrontés à un mouvement de radicalisation
en architecture et en urbanisation. Les théories révolu-
tionnaires de groupes comme Archigram, en Grande-
Bretagne, Archizoom et Superstudio en Italie portèrent
la discussion sur un terrain nouveau.

A la fin de la décennie, une polarisation du débat
devint évidente. Un lobby anti-design de plus en plus
influent tournait en dérision l'idée du «bon goût», de la
perfection formelle des modernistes et souhaitait plutôt
explorer les champs complexes et métaphoriques du
langage du design. Le conflit explosa avec la fermeture
par les contestataires de la Triennale de Milan en 1968.
Les ambitions des classicistes affrontaient celles des

Special issue of "Life" magazine, commemorating the moon
landing, 1969

detailed exploration and analysis. It is the author's intention, rather, to provide some broad suggestions which may prove helpful in coming to grips with the complexities of style and design in a decade surrounded an aura of myth and romance which makes it so uniquely cherished in our century.

in den frühen sechziger Jahren vorherrschende Optimismus und die darauf folgende Ernüchterung forderten eine radikale Diskussion über Architektur und Städteplanung. Architekten- und Designergruppen wie Archigram in England oder Archizoom und Superstudio in Italien stießen mit ihren provokanten Theorien und Projekten in völliges Neuland vor.

Gegen Ende der sechziger Jahre polarisierte sich die Design-Debatte zunehmend. Der Glaube an den guten Geschmack und an eine modernistische Formvollendung wurde von der immer lauter werdenden Anti-Design-Lobby, die sich lieber mit den Metaphern und der Vielschichtigkeit der Formensprache beschäftigte, verspottet. Der Konflikt erreichte 1968 mit der Besetzung der XV. Mailänder Triennale seinen Höhepunkt. Es war ein Interessenkonflikt zwischen Traditionalisten und Ikonoklasten. Die Designgeschichte der sechziger Jahre verdeutlicht, daß zwei gegensätzliche Positionen nicht nur nebeneinander existieren können, sondern beide die andere als Kontrast und Reibungsfläche benötigen.

"Nothing Personal", book of photographs by Richard Avedon, designed by **Marvin Israel**, 1964

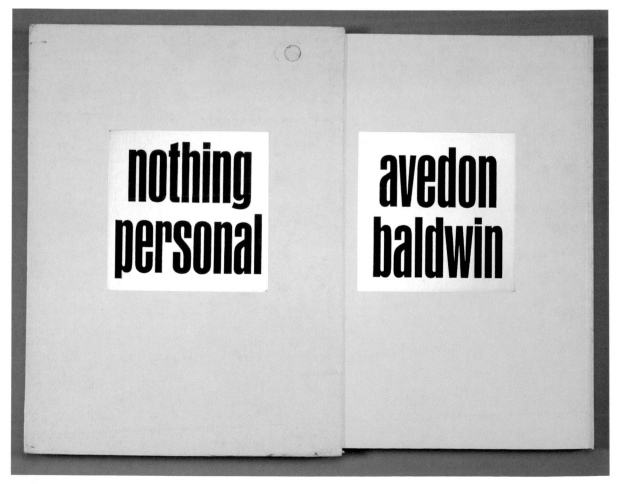

Im folgenden sollen diese gegensätzlichen Strömungen näher untersucht werden. Im Rahmen der hier vorliegenden, eher knappen Untersuchung war es leider nicht möglich, allen Aspekten gleichmäßig gerecht zu werden. Der Autor bittet deshalb wegen der vielen Auslassungen und der nur kurzen Hinweise auf die vielen künstlerischen Talente, die alle einer näheren Untersuchung und Analyse wert gewesen wären, um Nachsicht. Dieses Buch will in erster Linie Anregungen vermitteln, die dem interessierten Leser bei der Auseinandersetzung mit Stil und Design der sechziger Jahre helfen sollen – eines Jahrzehnts, das sich durch seine Aura von Mythik und Romantik in unserem Jahrhundert so großer Beliebtheit erfreut.

iconoclastes: pourtant, l'histoire du design des années soixante montre à plusieurs reprises que non seulement ces contraires peuvent coexister mais qu'ils se mettent en valeur l'un l'autre.

Voici donc certains des fils que nous suivrons ici. Le cadre restreint de cet essai excluant une présentation exhaustive du sujet, le lecteur voudra bien excuser des omissions ou de trop brèves références à des talents qui eussent mérité que l'on s'attardât davantage. L'auteur a cherché à dégager les grandes lignes permettant d'avoir une idée de la complexité de ce que furent style et design tout au long d'une décennie un peu magique qui nous apparaît maintenant comme un moment privilégié de notre siècle.

"Disraeli Gears", album cover for Cream, designed by **Martin Sharp** with a photograph by Bob Whitaker, 1967

The long and complex story of the Modern Movement can be traced back through the 19th century to the emergence of a school of thought that recognised the need to ally design theory with technical possibilities. The first great machine age inspired engineer architects and designers on a heroic scale. Men such as Joseph Paxton, architect of the Crystal Palace for the 1851 Great Exhibition in London; Isambard Kingdom Brunel, builder of the steamship The Great Eastern; Viollet-le-Duc, the great French architect; and Gustave Eiffel, visionary architect of the Tower which bears his name, set an alternative agenda to the Academy or Beaux-Arts traditions. These were the precursors of Modernism. In the 20th century, the multi-disciplinary art and design school, the Bauhaus, played the central role in defining Modernist principles.

The Bauhaus was closed by the Nazis in 1933. As early as 1932, the American architect Philip Johnson, who was to play so important a role in redefining Modernism in the post-war decades, had organised the first American exhibition on the subject. The exhibition, "The International Style", at New York's Museum of Modern Art (MoMA), established a crucial bridge between the ideals of Europe's most avant-garde design school and the power structure of the American design scene, dominated by the influence of corporate financing and the aesthetic elitism of the curatorial world.

Johnson was director of the department of architecture at MoMA from 1930 to 1936 and from 1946 to 1964. He established his own practice in New York in 1954 and four years later, in collaboration with Bauhaus émigré Mies van der Rohe, designed the Seagram Building on Park Avenue. This glass and bronze monolithic grid structure epitomised the International Style and became a template for the steel and glass skyscrapers which came to dominate the downtown areas of most major American cities over the next twenty years. The International Style adapted functionalist principles to create a style that spoke of self-confident authority. This was the style of Big Business, the utopian ideals of the original Bauhaus philosophers usurped by corporate America.

The International Style, predicated on rationalist principles, became the bearer of implicit messages that had much to do with status, prestige and power. The new rationalists were, in so many cases, planning a dream territory to express a new order emerging in the financial boom years after the war. By 1960 the pared-down style was dominating all areas of corporate, contract and domestic design. Contemporary journals and anthologies of the best of modern design focused on schemes for public and private spaces which had the simplicity and refinement of traditional Japanese interiors, a Zen sense of discipline, logic, grace and transcendental order. Clean lines and grids

Die lange und komplexe Geschichte der modernen Reformbewegung kann bis in das 19. Jahrhundert zurückverfolgt werden. Damals erkannte man die Notwendigkeit, die Gestaltungslehre mit den technischen Neuerungen in Einklang zu bringen. Das beginnende Maschinenzeitalter inspirierte Ingenieure, Architekten und Designer zu enormen Leistungen. Männer wie Joseph Paxton, der Schöpfer des Kristallpalastes für die Weltausstellung 1851 in London, Isambard Kingdom Brunel, der Konstrukteur des Dampfschiffes The Great Eastern, Viollet-le-Duc, der berühmte französische Architekt, und Gustave Eiffel, der visionäre Erbauer des nach ihm benannten Turms in Paris, wiesen neue Lösungen auf, die konträr zu den überholten Traditionen der Kunstschulen und Akademien standen. Sie waren die Pioniere des Modernismus. Im 20. Jahrhundert übernahm das Bauhaus in seiner Funktion als interdisziplinäre Kunst- und Designschule die entscheidende Rolle bei der Definition modernistischer Gestaltungsprinzipien.

Das Bauhaus wurde 1933 von den Nationalsozialisten geschlossen. Bereits 1932 organisierte der amerikanische Architekt Philip Johnson die erste amerikanische Ausstellung zum Internationalen Stil. Die Ausstellung »The International Style« im Museum of Modern Art in New York schuf eine dauerhafte Verbindung zwischen den Idealen der avantgardistischsten Designschule Europas und der amerikanischen Design-Szene, deren Machtstruktur vom Einfluß des kapitalkräftigen Unternehmertums und von dem elitären Geschmack der Museumskuratorien geprägt wurde.

Johnson leitete von 1930 bis 1936 und von 1946 bis 1964 die Architekturabteilung am Museum of Modern Art. 1954 gründete er in New York sein eigenes Architekturbüro. Vier Jahre später entwarf er in Zusammenarbeit mit dem emigrierten, ehemaligen Bauhaus-Direktor Mies van der Rohe das Seagram Building an der Park Avenue. Das Gebäude mit seiner monolithischen Rasterkonstruktion aus Glas und Bronze wurde zum Inbegriff des Internationalen Stils und hatte Vorbildcharakter für die zahlreichen Wolkenkratzer aus Stahl und Glas, die in den folgenden zwanzig Jahren in den Zentren der meisten amerikanischen Großstädte entstehen sollten. Der Internationale Stil adaptierte die Prinzipien des Funktionalismus, was ihm eine Ausstrahlung von Selbstsicherheit und Autorität verlieh: Es war der Stil des »Big Business«. Das Amerika der Industriekonzerne hatte sich der utopischen Ideale der Bauhaus-Philosophie bemächtigt.

Der auf rationalen Prinzipien basierende Internationale Stil wurde zum visuellen Träger von verdeckten Botschaften, die viel mit Status, Prestige und Macht zu tun hatten. Ab 1960 dominierte der sachliche Stil alle Gestaltungsbereiche der Industrie-, Büro- und Wohnlandschaft. Zeitgenössische Designzeitschriften und Fachpublikationen konzentrierten sich auf die Veröffentlichung solcher öffentlicher und privater Inneneinrichtungen, die die Einfachheit und Kultiviertheit traditioneller japanischer

La longue et complexe histoire du Mouvement moderne a ses racines au 19ème siècle. Il découle d'un courant de pensée qui part de la nécessité de rapprocher les théories du design des nouvelles possibilités techniques. Le premier grand âge des machines inspira des créations héroïques à des architectes et à des designers comme Joseph Paxton, créateur du Crystal Palace, Isambard Kingdom Brunel, constructeur du navire à vapeur The Great Eastern, Viollet-le-Duc, grand architecte français, et Gustave Eiffel, visionnaire, père de la tour du même nom. Ces hommes ont tous su imposer une alternative au programme traditionnel de l'Académie ou des Beaux-Arts, et sont les précurseurs du Modernisme. Au 20ème siècle, c'est le Bauhaus, école multi-disciplinaire d'art et de design, qui joue un rôle prédominant dans la définition des principes du Mouvement.

Le Bauhaus fut interdit par les nazis en 1933. Dès 1932, l'architecte américain Philip Johnson, qui allait jouer un rôle de première importance dans la refonte du Modernisme de l'après-guerre, avait organisé dans son pays la première exposition sur le sujet. Elle eut lieu à New York, au Museum of Modern Art (MoMA) sous le titre «The International Style» et servit de pont entre les idéaux de l'avant-garde européenne et le paysage du design américain qui se trouvait sous une double influence, celle, financière, du monde des affaires et celle, esthétique, de l'élite des conservateurs de musée.

Johnson fut directeur du département d'architecture du MoMA de 1930 à 1936 et de 1946 à 1964. Il fonda sa propre agence à New York en 1954 et quatre ans plus tard, en collaboration avec un émigré du Bauhaus, Mies van der Rohe, il créa le Seagram Building sur Park Avenue. Cette structure monolithique de verre et de bronze devint le flambeau du Style International et le modèle des gratte-ciel qui allaient se dresser au cœur des grandes villes américaines dans les vingt années à venir. Il s'agissait, à partir de principes fonctionnalistes, de créer des bâtiments donnant une impression de rassurante autorité. Tel était le style du «big business»: l'Amérique des affaires avait repris à son compte les idées des pionniers du Bauhaus.

Le Style International, sur la base de principes rationalistes, véhiculait des messages implicites, expressions de statut, de prestige et de pouvoir. Dans bien des cas, les nouveaux rationalistes préparaient un territoire idéal où ils pourraient exprimer un ordre nouveau, né de la croissance économique de l'après-guerre. En 1960, ce style, dans sa plus simple expression, régnait en maître dans tous les domaines, professionnel, public et privé, du design. Magazines et anthologies spécialisés de l'époque présentent des projets qui ont la simplicité et le raffinement d'intérieurs japonais traditionnels et qui témoignent d'un sens zen de la discipline, de logique, d'harmonie et d'ordre transcendantal. Les lignes pures, les formes géométriques de l'architecture trouvent leur complément dans un ameublement qui reflète «une

2

The Rationalists – International Modernism

Die Rationalisten – Internationaler Modernismus

Les Rationalistes – Modernisme International

TOP
Hans and Florence Knoll

BOTTOM
Poster for Knoll International,
designed by **Massimo Vignelli**,
1967

in architecture were complemented by furnishings reflecting "Logical thinking … combined with an understanding of tools, machines and materials to achieve simply an aesthetically satisfying solution" (Dennis & Barbara Young, *furniture in britain today*, London, 1964, preface).

The Sixties offered designers the opportunity to focus on new spaces: the airport lounges and concourses, the corporate headquarters with their lobbies, boardrooms and open-plan office spaces which defined a new age of international jet travel and booming business. The most powerful countries of the capitalist world were redefining the idea of colonisation in terms of the outreach of financial and service industries; micro-technology was creating a new machine age, the light industries catering to a vast, increasingly affluent middle class hungry for new domestic gadgetry.

A small number of firms and design groups dominated the fields of contract and product design. Foremost amongst the new rationalists were the American companies Knoll Associates Inc. and Herman Miller. Founded in 1937, Knoll came to prominence through the fifties under the leadership of Hans and Florence Schust Knoll and by the turn of the decade was foremost in promoting a look which embraced the best of purist pre-war Bauhaus Modernism and the finest contemporary design. Knoll gave birth to the notion of "classic" modern designs by re-issuing furniture by Marcel Breuer and Mies van der Rohe alongside new designs in a similar vein. Florence Knoll's elegant cabinets in steel, marble and wood or laminate were an expression of Modernism at its most pure. Knoll and Herman Miller invested considerable design resources in the creation of state-of-the-art office systems with a new set of requirements appropriate to the mood of the Sixties. Highly flexible, open-plan systems designed on ergonomic principles brought a sense of enlightenment to the workplace. Herman Miller developed their pioneering, versatile "Action Office"; Knoll countered with their own ranges and strengthened their position in this market by focusing simultaneously on the design issues of creating corporate identities.

These companies' concerns were characteristic of an international pattern, expressed, for example, in Great Britain in the work of the firm of Hille, whose leading designer, Robin Day, proved a master of the new Modernism, and, in Germany, in the Büro Landschaft research. The Büro Landschaft project, led by Eberhardt and Wolfgang Schnelle of the Hamburg-based Quickborner team, involved the analysis of interaction patterns and proposed organic, open-plan office "landscapes" with an emphasis on design as a process of facilitating communication as well as creating physical forms. In Italy, the typewriter and office

Interieurs ausstrahlten und einen an der Zenphilosophie orientierten Sinn für Disziplin, Logik, Anmut und transzendentale Ordnung erkennen ließen. Den klaren Linien und Rastern der Architektur entsprachen die Möblierungen, in denen sich »logisches Denken … mit dem Verständnis für Werkzeug, Maschinen und Materialien verband, um eine ästhetisch zufriedenstellende Lösung zu erreichen« (Dennis & Barbara Young, »furniture in britain today«, London 1964, Vorwort).

Den Designern bot sich in den sechziger Jahren die Chance, sich mit neuen Raumverhältnissen auseinanderzusetzen. Die Clubräume und Wartehallen von Flughäfen, die Verwaltungsgebäude der Großkonzerne mit ihren Eingangshallen, Vorstandszimmern und Großraumbüros wurden zu Symbolen einer neuen Zeit, in der internationale Flugreisen an der Tagesordnung waren und wirtschaftliche Hochkonjunktur herrschte. Die mächtigsten Länder der kapitalistischen Welt vollzogen durch die weltweite Vernetzung ihrer Finanz- und Dienstleistungsunternehmen eine zweite Kolonisierung. Mit der Mikrotechnologie brach ein neues Maschinenzeitalter an. Die Leichtindustrie versorgte eine immer größer und wohlhabender werdende Mittelschicht, die auf die neuen Elektrogeräte für den Haushalt versessen war.

Das Büro- und Industriedesign wurde von einer kleinen Anzahl von Firmen und Designergruppen dominiert. Führend auf dem Gebiet des rationalen Wohnstils waren die amerikanischen Firmen Knoll Associates Inc. und Herman Miller. Unter der Leitung von Hans und Florence Knoll (geb. Schust) erlangte die 1937 gegründete Firma Knoll schon in den fünfziger Jahren weltweite Bedeutung. Ende des Jahrzehnts übernahm die Firma dann die Vorreiterrolle in der Propagierung eines Wohnstils, der den puristischen Bauhaus-Modernismus der Vorkriegsjahre mit dem besten zeitgenössischen Design verband. Knoll kreierte den »klassischen« modernen Wohnstil, indem die Firma Möbel nach Entwürfen von Marcel Breuer und Mies van der Rohe neu auflegte und gleichzeitig moderne, gleichgesinnte Entwürfe produzierte. In den Firmen Knoll und Herman Miller wurde mit Hochdruck an der Entwicklung moderner Büromöbelsysteme gearbeitet. Die nach ergonomischen Grundsätzen konstruierten, äußerst variablen Großraum-Büromöbelsysteme vermittelten ein Gefühl der Weite und ließen den Arbeitsplatz heller und freundlicher erscheinen. Bei Herman Miller wurde das zukunftsweisende und vielseitige Büromöbelsystem »Action Office« entwickelt; die Firma Knoll reagierte ihrerseits mit der Produktion eigener Büromöbelsysteme und verstärkte zusätzlich ihre Wettbewerbsfähigkeit, indem sie gestalterische Lösungen zur Schaffung von »Corporate Identities« anbot.

Daß die Vorgehensweise dieser beiden Firmen dem internationalen Trend entsprach, belegt die Tätigkeit der englischen Firma Hille. Ihr bekanntester Designer, Robin Day, galt als Meister des modernistischen Stils. Auch in

réflexion logique combinée à une compréhension des moyens techniques, des machines et des matériaux, dans le simple but d'obtenir une solution esthétiquement satisfaisante.» (Dennis & Barbara Young, «furniture in britain today», Londres, 1964, Préface.)

Les années soixante offrirent de nouveaux espaces à l'imagination des designers, salles d'attente des aéroports, quartiers généraux des grandes entreprises avec leurs salles de réception, leurs salles de réunion et leurs bureaux ouverts, terrains nouveaux de l'ère de communications ultrarapides et de grande expansion économique. Les plus puissants pays du monde capitaliste redéfinissaient la notion de colonisation en termes d'expansion du domaine des services financiers et administratifs. La micro-technologie donnait naissance à un nouvel âge de la machine et les industries légères approvisionnaient une classe moyenne de plus en plus aisée, avide de gadgets.

Un nombre restreint de firmes dominait le marché du design, design de contrat ou design de produit. Tête de file des nouveaux rationalistes, les entreprises américaines Knoll Associates Inc. et Herman Miller. Fondé en 1937, Knoll connut son essor tout au long des années cinquante sous l'égide de Hans et Florence Knoll (née Schust) et, à la fin de cette décennie, était devenu le premier représentant d'un style qui combinait ce qu'il y avait de meilleur dans le Modernisme puriste du Bauhaus d'avant-guerre et dans le design contemporain haut de gamme. En rééditant des meubles de Marcel Breuer et Mies van der Rohe, et en lançant en même temps des créations nouvelles d'une facture comparable, Knoll inventa la notion de design moderne «classique». Les élégants meubles à rangement de Florence Knoll, faits d'acier, de marbre et de bois ou de laminé, étaient une expression d'un Modernisme à son plus haut degré de pureté. Knoll et Herman Miller investissent des ressources considérables dans la création d'un aménagement adapté aux bureaux et aux besoins de l'époque. Des plans aux vastes espaces, d'une grande flexibilité, tracés selon des principes ergonomiques, donnaient à la notion de lieu de travail un relief nouveau. Avec l'«Action Office», Herman Miller créa une structure originale, modulable. Knoll répliqua avec ses propres objets et affirma sa position en s'appliquant également à créer une image de marque propre à chaque client.

Ces firmes représentaient une tendance internationale. En Grande-Bretagne, par exemple, les mêmes principes furent appliqués par Hille, dont le créateur principal, Robin Day, se révéla un maître du nouveau modernisme, et, en Allemagne par Büro Landschaft, qui menait un important travail de recherche. Le projet de Büro Landschaft, mené par Eberhardt et Wolfgang Schnelle de l'équipe Quickborner, de Hambourg, consistait en une analyse des schémas d'interaction et proposait des «bureaux-paysages» ouverts et organiques où le design était destiné à faciliter la communication tout autant

Office in the President's Suite in the C. B. S. building in New York, designed by **Florence Knoll**, 1964, incorporating her credenza design of 1961

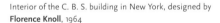

Interior of the C. B. S. building in New York, designed by **Florence Knoll**, 1964

Mobil

Mobil logo, designed by
Tom Geismar of Chermayeff
& Geismar Inc, 1964

furniture and machinery manufacturer Olivetti set a standard for applying high design principles and a comprehensive design programme, paying equal attention to every area of their business, from the products and their packaging and advertising to the corporate image. Mario Bellini, Marcello Nizzoli and Ettore Sottsass contributed in various ways to Olivetti's market leadership. The Milan design practice BBPR played an important role in promoting Modernist ideas, working with numerous clients including Olivetti.

Corporate identities and house styles became important branches of design practice in the Sixties as companies recognised the need to maximise their image in the market place. Dynamic logos and rationalised typography became a new focus of attention for designers, a new speciality in the modern market place. American graphic designer Paul Rand had set a standard with his work for IBM since the fifties. The London design group of Fletcher, Forbes and Gill brought clarity, intelligence and humour to this discipline.

The world and the market place had changed out of all recognition since the pioneer years of Modernism. Utopian ideals gave way to market forces and the Bauhaus philosophy was developed into the high-profile International Style. The school's closure, however, left a gap in German design which was to be filled by the establishment in 1955 of the Hochschule für Gestaltung (HfG) at Ulm. This new design school was founded by Grete and Inge Scholl with Max Bill as director. Bill was a Swiss architect and designer who had studied at the Bauhaus and provided a link between the pioneering school and its successor at Ulm. He was the most rigorous minimalist in his application of rationalist principles, and made his mark on German industrial design as well as within the field of typography and graphics. Bill more than any other made the label "Swiss" synonymous with a rigorous, uncluttered approach to design through the fifties, Sixties and Seventies.

The avowed aim of the Hochschule für Gestaltung was to revive and develop the work of the Bauhaus, most specifically in applying rationalist research, development and design principles to German industry. The HfG is perhaps best known for its close working relationship with Braun, the manufacturer of electrical goods. Braun, under the guidance of Artur Braun, one of the founder's sons, recruited designers from the HfG, notably Dr. Fritz Eichler and Hans Gugelot, who, with Dieter Rams and Otl Aicher, made Braun products synonymous with formal, purist design. In 1964, New York's MoMA hosted an exhibition of Braun products, consecrating in this temple of Modernism the cult of the minimalist aesthetic.

Tomás Maldonado's researches at Ulm explored a

Deutschland experimentierte man auf dem Gebiet der Büromöbelausstattung. Das Projekt »Bürolandschaft«, unter der Leitung von Eberhardt und Wolfgang Schnelle vom Hamburger »Quickborn Team«, verarbeitete in den von ihnen geplanten organischen Großraum-Bürolandschaften die Analyse von Interaktionsmustern. In Italien setzte die Firma Olivetti als Produzent von Schreib- und Büromaschinen sowie von Büromöbeln auf der Suche nach hohen Design-Standards und einer einheitlichen Formensprache neue Maßstäbe. Dabei wurde allen Geschäftsbereichen, ausgehend von der Warenproduktion über deren Verpackung und Vermarktung bis hin zur Schaffung einer Corporate Identity, die gleiche Aufmerksamkeit gewidmet. Designer wie Mario Bellini, Marcello Nizzoli und Ettore Sottsass trugen, jeder auf seine Weise, zur Position Olivettis als Marktführer bei. Dem in Mailand ansässigen Design-Büro BBPR, das nicht nur für Olivetti, sondern auch für zahlreiche andere Kunden tätig wurde, kam bei der Verbreitung modernistischer Ideen eine zentrale Funktion zu.

Als die Unternehmen in den sechziger Jahren die Notwendigkeit erkannten, ihr Image am Markt zu verbessern, wurde Corporate Identity, also die Schaffung eines bestimmten »Firmenstils«, zu einem wichtigen Betätigungsfeld von Designern. Der Entwurf dynamischer Firmenlogos und rationalisierter Typographien stand dabei im Mittelpunkt der Interessen und führte zu einer neuen Spezialisierung im Bereich der Absatzstrategie. Bereits seit den fünfziger Jahren setzte der amerikanische Grafiker Paul Rand mit seiner Tätigkeit für die Firma IBM neue Maßstäbe. Die in London ansässige Designergruppe Fletcher, Forbes und Gill führte Klarheit, Intelligenz und Humor in den Bereich des Graphik-Designs ein.

Welt und Wirtschaft hatten sich seit den Anfängen der Moderne stark verändert. Utopische Ideale waren den Erfordernissen der Marktwirtschaft gewichen. Aus der Bauhaus-Philsophie hatte sich der hochprofilierte Internationale Stil entwickelt. In Deutschland war mit der Schließung des Bauhauses eine Lücke im Bereich der Designlehre entstanden, die erst 1955 durch die von Grete und Inge Scholl gegründete Hochschule für Gestaltung in Ulm gefüllt werden konnte. Erster Direktor dieser neuen Designschule wurde Max Bill. Der Schweizer Architekt und Designer hatte noch am Bauhaus studiert und fungierte so als Bindeglied zwischen der ursprünglichen Schule und der Nachfolgeinstitution in Ulm. Mehr als irgendein anderer sorgte Bill in den fünfziger, sechziger und siebziger Jahren dafür, daß der Begriff »schweizerisch« zum Synonym für ein strikt reduziertes Design wurde.

Erklärtes Ziel der Ulmer Hochschule für Gestaltung war die Wiederbelebung und Weiterführung der Bauhaus-Arbeit, was sich insbesondere auf die Kooperation mit der deutschen Industrie in bezug auf die Anwendung rationalistischer Forschungs-, Entwicklungs- und Design-

qu'à créer des formes. En Italie, le fabricant de machines à écrire et autres équipements de bureau, Olivetti, appliqua un programme de design exemplaire, accordant la même attention à toutes les phases de la production, depuis les produits eux-mêmes jusqu'à leur emballage, la publicité et l'image de marque de l'entreprise. Mario Bellini, Marcello Nizzoli et Ettore Sottsass eurent à divers titres une part de mérite dans le succès d'Olivetti sur le marché international. L'agence de design milanaise BBPR fut pour beaucoup dans la promotion d'idées modernistes et collabora à de nombreux projets, notamment au programme Olivetti.

Les compagnies devenant de plus en plus désireuses de se présenter avantageusement sur le marché, l'image de marque et le style particulier à l'entreprise devinrent des éléments importants de la pratique du design dans les années soixante. Les créateurs se penchèrent sur un point nouveau: les logos et la typographie coordonnée. Le graphiste américain Paul Rand et son travail pour IBM étaient, depuis les années cinquante, le point de référence. A Londres, le groupe Fletcher, Forbes et Gill apporta à cette discipline clarté, intelligence et humour.

Depuis l'époque des pionniers du modernisme, le monde et le marché s'étaient transformés. Les idéaux avaient cédé la place aux impératifs économiques et la philosophie du Bauhaus avait engendré le prestigieux Style International. Pourtant, la fermeture de cette école avait laissé un vide dans le monde du design allemand qui sera comblé par la fondation, en 1955, par Grete et Inge Scholl de l'Ecole de design d'Ulm dont Max Bill devint le directeur. Bill était un architecte et designer suisse qui avait fait ses études au Bauhaus et pouvait donc maintenir le lien entre cet établissement-pionnier et la nouvelle école d'Ulm. Minimaliste à l'extrême dans son interprétation des principes rationalistes, il marqua de son sceau le design industriel allemand de même que les domaines du graphisme et de la typographie. Plus que tout autre, Bill contribua à ce que le mot «suisse» fût synonyme, tout au long des années cinquante, soixante et soixante-dix, de rigueur et d'ascétisme.

Le but avoué de l'école d'Ulm était de faire revivre et de prolonger le travail du Bauhaus, plus particulièrement en appliquant à l'industrie allemande des principes de recherche rationnelle, de développement et de design. C'est sans doute sa collaboration avec la firme Braun, fabricant d'appareils électriques, qui est l'illustration la plus réussie de ce programme. Braun, sous l'impulsion de son directeur Artur Braun, un des fils du fondateur, fit appel à des designers de l'école, notamment au Dr Fritz Eichler et à Hans Gugelot qui, avec Dieter Rams et Otl Aicher, firent des produits Braun les symboles d'un design d'une grande pureté formelle. En 1964, le MoMA, à New York, en présenta une exposition: le culte de l'esthétique minimaliste fut consacré dans le temple du Modernisme.

A Ulm, les recherches de Tomás Maldonado se portè-

Promotional motif for Olivetti, designed by **Giovanni Pintori**, late 1960s

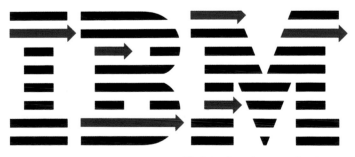

IBM logo, late 60s variant, designed by **Robert Paganucci**, of the versatile logo created by Paul Rand in 1956

The Rationalists – International Modernism **23**

more abstract set of problems. Communication and sign systems were foremost amongst his concerns. The introduction to an anthology of his writings (*Uppercase* 5, 1961, edited by Theo Crosby) describes "a vision of the New Jerusalem, that *Ville Radieuse*, that already exists in fragments in the writings and the works of the many great, but isolated men of our time. Our task is to build these fragments into a civilization, based on the servitude of the machine: mass production, mass communication, mass participation". Here was the succinct translation of Walter Gropius's founding Bauhaus ideals into the language of the age of mass culture.

Central to the rationalist cause was the public acceptance of a concept of "good" design sponsored by industry, museums or the state. The Museum of Modern Art's departments of architecture and design, shaped by Philip Johnson, Edgar Kaufmann Jr. and Arthur Drexler, added authority to the purist school by the emphasis within their collecting and exhibition programmes. Britain's Design Centre, opened in 1956 under the sponsorship of the Council of Industrial Design, served a comparable educational role, fighting the cause, not without bias, of "good" design. The *Compasso d'Oro* awards, sponsored by the Milan department store *La Rinascente* since 1954, and the *Gute Form* exhibitions, organised in Germany by Max Bill, spotlit design achievements. These institutional pursuits of a definition of "good" design tended to favour clean-lined functionalism over expressive styling or metaphor. International Modernism put rationalist, minimalist aesthetics centre-stage as an Establishment mode.

The Scandinavian strand of Modernism had its own identity and reached out to a broad international market in the Fifties and Sixties. The Scandinavian countries had a strong tradition of harmonisation between craft standards and series production; and Scandinavian Modernism has always enjoyed a reputation for tempering the cool extremes of minimalist designs with a respect for the tactile qualities of natural materials, particularly native woods. An underlying respect for truth to materials and a concern to give pleasure to the user have given Scandinavian design an international reputation for logic and warmth. The Danish designer Poul Kjaerholm was among the most rigorous, yet tempered his simple forms by judiciously mixing warm natural materials with the ubiquitous steel and marble of Modernism. Danish product designer Arne Jacobsen gave tremendous grace to his creations without compromising the most strict expression of the Modernist aesthetic.

Rationalism was given a novel twist in Italy with characteristic flair by designers developing new forms for new materials. The firm of Kartell employed a group of experimental designers including Anna

prinzipien auswirkte. Die Hochschule für Gestaltung wurde berühmt durch ihre enge Zusammenarbeit mit der Elektrofirma Braun AG. Unter der Leitung von Artur Braun, einem der Söhne des Firmengründers, war es zu ersten Kontakten zwischen der Braun AG und Designern der Ulmer Hochschule gekommen, allen voran Dr. Fritz Eichler und Hans Gugelot. Zusammen mit Dieter Rams und Otl Aicher kommt ihnen das Verdienst zu, daß Erzeugnisse der Firma Braun zum Inbegriff des formalen, puristischen Designs wurden. 1964 organisierte das Museum of Modern Art in New York eine Ausstellung mit Produkten der Firma Braun: Der Kult der minimalistischen Ästhetik war in den Tempel der Moderne eingezogen.

Die Ulmer Forschungen von Tomás Maldonado betrafen dagegen eine Reihe abstrakterer Probleme. Maldonados Hauptinteresse galt der Entwicklung von Kommunikations- und Zeichensystemen. Im Vorwort zu einer Anthologie seiner Schriften (»Uppercase 5«, 1961, herausgegeben von Theo Crosby) wird die »Vision des Neuen Jerusalems, jener ›Ville Radieuse‹, die vereinzelt bereits in den Schriften und Werken vieler berühmter Persönlichkeiten unseres Jahrhunderts ablesbar ist«, beschrieben. Weiter heißt es dort: »Es ist unsere Aufgabe diese Fragmente in den Dienst einer Zivilisation zu stellen, die auf der Ausnutzung der Maschine beruht: Es geht um Massenproduktion, Massenkommunikation und Massenpartizipation.« Hier sind die von Walter Gropius anläßlich der Bauhaus-Gründung formulierten Ideale prägnant in die Sprache eines multikulturellen Zeitalters übersetzt worden.

Den Rationalisten lag sehr viel daran, daß ihr von der Industrie, den Museen und vom Staat gefördertes Konzept vom »guten Design« auch von der breiten Öffentlichkeit akzeptiert wurde. Die Architektur- und Designabteilungen des Museum of Modern Art, die weitgehend unter dem Einfluß von Philip Johnson, Edgar Kaufmann Jr. und Arthur Drexler standen, stärkten durch die Gewichtung ihrer Ausstellungs- und Sammeltätigkeit den Bekanntheitsgrad des puristischen Designs. Eine vergleichbare Rolle, wenngleich nicht ganz ohne Vorbehalte gegenüber dem »guten Design«, übernahm das britische Design Centre, das 1956 mit Unterstützung des Council of Industrial Design eröffnet worden war. Auch die von dem Mailänder Kaufhaus »La Rinascente« seit 1954 verliehene Auszeichnung »Compasso d'Oro« und die von Max Bill in Deutschland organisierten Ausstellungen unter dem Motto »Die Gute Form« stellten die Leistungen von Designern in den Blickpunkt der Öffentlichkeit. Alle diese institutionellen Beiträge zur Definition des »guten Designs« neigten jedoch dazu, dem Funktionalismus mit seinen klaren Linien gegenüber einer expressiven Gestaltung den Vorzug zu geben. Der internationale Modernismus rückte die funktionale, minimalistische Ästhetik in den Mittelpunkt des Geschmacks des Establishments.

Braun "Cylindric" cigarette lighter, designed by **Dieter Rams**, 1968

rent sur un aspect plus abstrait de la question. Ce qui l'occupait avant tout, c'était la communication et la sémiotique. Dans l'introduction à une anthologie de ses écrits («Uppercase» 5, 1961, éditée par Theo Crosby) il décrit «une vision de la Nouvelle Jérusalem, cette ‹Ville Radieuse› qui existe dans les écrits et les œuvres de bien des hommes éminents, mais si isolés, de notre temps. Notre travail est de refondre ces efforts fragmentés en une civilisation basée sur l'utilisation de la machine pour une production de masse, une communication de masse, une participation de masse.» On retrouve ici les principes fondateurs du Bauhaus de Walter Gropius, traduits dans un langage qui est celui de l'ère de la culture de masse.

"Uppercase 5", edited by Theo Crosby, with an essay by Tomás Maldonado, 1961

Le nerf de la cause rationaliste était la notion communément admise d'un «bon» design, promu par l'industrie, les musées et l'Etat. Les départements d'architecture et de design du Museum of Modern Art, New York, mis en place par Philip Johnson, Edgar Kaufmann Jr. et Arthur Drexler, apportèrent, par leurs acquisitions et leurs programmes d'exposition, un soutien accru à l'école puriste. En Grande-Bretagne, le Design Centre, fondé en 1956 sous l'égide du Council of International Design, poursuivait le même but pédagogique et défendait, non sans parti pris, la cause du «bon» design. Un «Compasso d'Oro» offert par le grand magasin milanais «La Rinascente» depuis 1954 et les expositions «Die Gute Form» organisées par Max Bill, en Allemagne, faisaient connaître au public les créations de cette discipline. Toutes ces sanctions officielles tendirent à favoriser un fonctionnalisme aux lignes pures au détriment d'un style expressif ou métaphorique. Le mouvement Moderniste international mit l'esthétique rationaliste et minimaliste sous les feux de la rampe et en fit le style de l'«Establishment».

La version scandinave du Modernisme avait son identité propre et touchait, dans les années cinquante et soixante, un vaste marché international. Traditionnellement, les Scandinaves s'entendaient à concilier exigences de l'artisanat et fabrication en série, et le style scandinave moderne avait toujours eu la réputation de savoir tempérer un minimalisme radical par les qualités tactiles de matériaux naturels, le bois, surtout. Ce respect sous-jacent des qualités du matériau ainsi que le désir de procurer du plaisir à l'utilisateur ont assuré au design scandinave une réputation de logique et de convivialité. Le Danois Poul Kjaerholm, un des créateurs les plus rigoureux, sut adoucir ses formes simples en combinant avec le marbre et l'acier, incontournables, des matériaux chauds et naturels. Arne Jacobsen, Danois lui aussi, créa des produits pleins d'allure sans pour cela compromettre les règles esthétiques modernistes.

Les tenants italiens du rationalisme, avec leur perspicacité proverbiale, surent donner un essor nouveau à la tendance et conçurent des formes nouvelles pour des matériaux nouveaux. La firme Kartell commanda à un

Braun "Sixtant SM 31" shaver, designed by **Hans Gugelot** and **G. A. Müller**, 1962

Design Centre award logo,
introduced in 1959

Castelli Ferrieri and Joe Colombo to devise new
furniture and object forms, to be made in injection-
moulded plastics. These brightly coloured sculptural
designs gave a distinctive Sixties identity to the Modernist principle of devising forms appropriate to the
very latest technology. A.B.S. injection-moulded plastic
was the tubular steel of its age, and the products
launched by Kartell and other manufacturers, including Danese and Artemide, represented the true
creative front line of Modernist design practice.

The Japanese contribution to the progress of Modernism was in the area of technological development
and in building an industrial base which was to have
a major impact in the world market for audio and
photo equipment, televisions and motor cars. Sony,
Panasonic, Nikon, Pentax, Toshiba and Honda became
leading brand names in the competitive international
markets for consumer hardware. Traditional Japanese
skills in miniaturisation and packaging, and high,
productive work standards, gave the new Japanese
industrial samurai their cutting edge.

In Skandinavien hatte sich eine individuelle Form des
Modernismus entwickelt, die in den fünfziger und sechziger Jahren auch international starke Beachtung fand.
Die skandinavischen Länder hatten es schon immer verstanden, handwerkliche Standards mit den Erfordernissen der Serienproduktion in Einklang zu bringen. Der
skandinavische Modernismus war dafür bekannt, daß er
die kalten Extreme des minimalistischen Designs durch
die Verwendung natürlicher, warmer Werkstoffe, insbesondere einheimischer Hölzer, milderte. Der dänische
Designer Poul Kjaerholm, einer der extremen Vertreter
des Funktionalismus, schwächte trotz strengster Formgebung die Wirkung von modernistischen Werkstoffen
wie Stahl und Marmor ab, indem er diese mit natürli-
chen, warmen Materialien kombinierte. Arne Jacobsen,
ein weiterer dänischer Industriedesigner, verlieh seinen
Entwürfen große Eleganz, ohne ihre streng modernistische Auffassung zu verfälschen.

In Italien erarbeiteten Designer neue Formen für neue
Werkstoffe, was dazu führte, daß der Rationalismus hier
eine eigene Ausprägung mit speziellem Flair erhielt. Die
Firma Kartell beschäftigte eine Reihe experimenteller
Designer, darunter auch Anna Castelli Ferrieri und Joe
Colombo. Sie erarbeiteten eine neue Formensprache für
Möbel und Objekte, die im Spritzgußverfahren aus
Kunststoff hergestellt werden konnten. In diesen leuch-
tend bunten, dreidimensionalen Objekten gewann das
modernistische Postulat, nach dem die Formgebung
stets dem neuesten Stand der Technologie entsprechen
sollte, eine für die sechziger Jahre typische, unverwech-
selbare Identität. Der für das Spritzgußverfahren geeig-
nete A.B.S.-Kunststoff war sozusagen das Stahlrohr dieses Zeitalters. Die von der Firma Kartell und anderen
Herstellern wie Danese und Artemide auf den Markt
gebrachten Produkte verkörperten herausragende
Designleistungen im Sinne des Modernismus, die ganz
auf der Höhe ihrer Zeit standen.

Japans Beitrag zum Fortschritt des Modernismus lag
im Bereich der technologischen Forschung. Hier wurden
die Grundlagen erarbeitet, die den weltweiten Markt der
Phono-, Foto-, Fernseh- und Autoindustrie erheblich in
Bewegung bringen sollte. Firmen wie Sony, Panasonic,
Nikon, Pentax, Toshiba und Honda übernahmen im
Bereich der Konsumgüterindustrie die internationale
Führung. Die traditionellen Fertigkeiten der Japaner in
bezug auf Miniaturisierungs- und Verpackungstechniken
in Kombination mit ihren hohen arbeits- und produkti-
onstechnischen Standards verhalfen den »Industrie-
Samurai« zum Durchbruch.

"Doney" television, designed
by **Marco Zanuso** and **Richard
Sapper**, 1962

groupe de créateurs expérimentaux, parmi lesquels Anna Castelli Ferrieri et Joe Colombo, des meubles et des objets qui seraient réalisés en plastique moulé. Ces formes colorées et sculpturales, très «années soixante», illustrent bien le principe moderniste selon lequel l'imagination doit utiliser les technologies de pointe. Le plastique moulé par injection devint l'acier tubulaire de l'époque et les produits lancés par Kartell et d'autres fabricants comme Danese et Artemide se retrouvèrent en première ligne de la pratique moderniste.

La contribution japonaise à l'évolution du Modernisme se fit dans les domaines du développement technologique et dans l'élaboration d'un programme industriel de base. Elle allait avoir un grand retentissement sur le marché mondial de l'équipement audiovisuel et de l'automobile. Sony, Panasonic, Nikon, Pentax, Toshiba et Honda devinrent têtes de file de la production de consommation. L'ingéniosité naturelle des Japonais dans le domaine de la miniaturisation et du packaging s'alliait à une grande rigueur en matière de production pour faire de ces samouraïs industriels les fines lames que l'on sait.

Sony's first solid-state television receiver, 1959

Kodak carousel projector, designed by **Reinhold Hocker** and **Hans Gugelot**, 1964

PAGES **28/29**
Knoll Los Angeles Showroom, designed by **Florence Knoll**, with Mies van der Rohe Barcelona chairs, Eero Saarinen tulip chairs and tables, 1960

Knoll "Bastiano" seating,
designed by **Tobia Scarpa**,
1969, used in an interior with
re-edited chairs designed in
the late 20s by **Marcel Breuer**

Hille "Form" seating,
designed by **Robin Day**,
introduced February 1960

Knoll board room with table
and chairs. The table designed
by **Florence Knoll**, 1961, the
chairs designed by **Charles
Pollock**, 1965

Knoll tables and sideboard,
designed by **Florence Knoll**,
1961

Herman Miller "Action Office", Series 1, introduced in 1964, designed by **Robert Propst** in cooperation with George Nelson, incorporating the chair designed by **Charles Eames**

Herman Miller "Action Office", incorporating the "Executive" chair, designed by **Charles Eames**

PAGE **33**
Herman Miller "Action Office", 1964–65

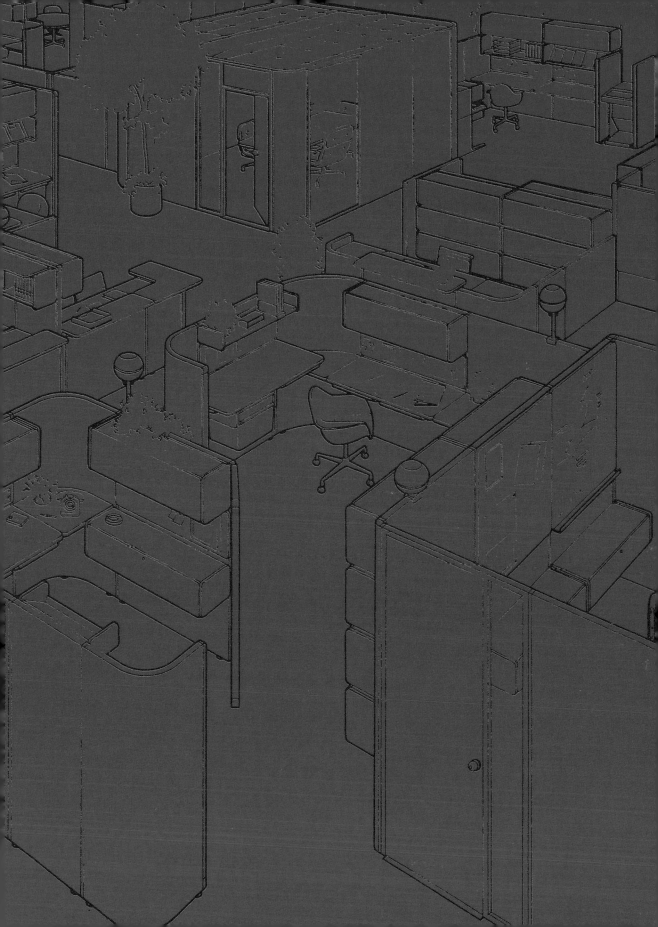

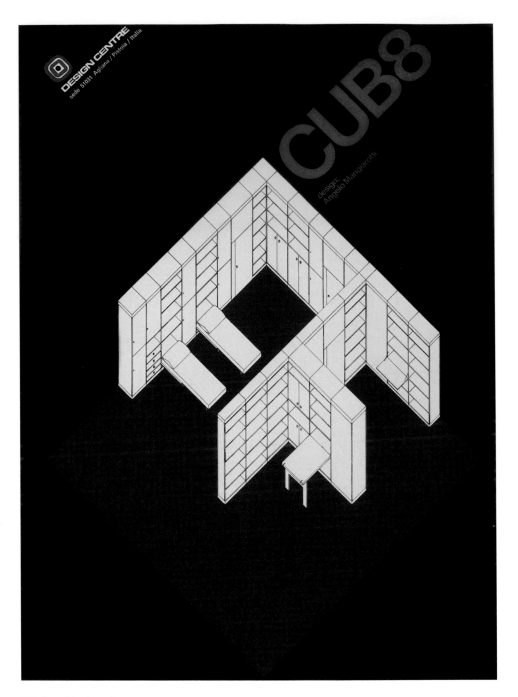

"Cub 8" modular domestic
units, designed by **Angelo
Mangiarotti**, advertisement
published 1969

PAGE **35** TOP
Olivetti office design, incorporating a desk designed by the
BBPR partnership, 1962,
advertisement published 1967

PAGE **35** BOTTOM
Desk, designed by the **BBPR
partnership**

The Rationalists – International Modernism **35**

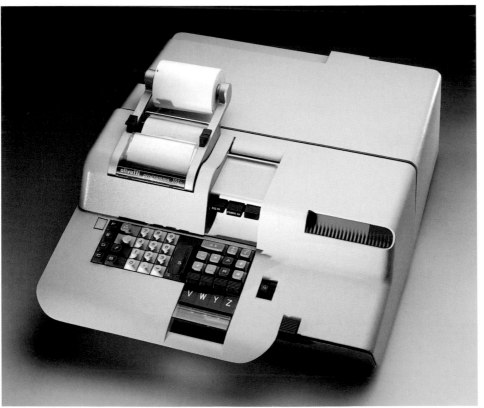

Olivetti "Praxis 48" typewriter,
designed by **Hans von Klier**
and **Ettore Sottsass Jr.**, 1964

Olivetti "Programma 1a"
calculator, designed by
Mario Bellini, 1965

Olivetti showroom in Paris, designed by **Gae Aulenti**, 1967

Olivetti TCV 250 terminal, designed by **Mario Bellini**, 1969

PAGES **38/39**
Foyer in the multi-storey office block for members of parliament in Bonn, designed by **Egon Eiermann**, 1968, with the "620" armchair designed by **Dieter Rams**

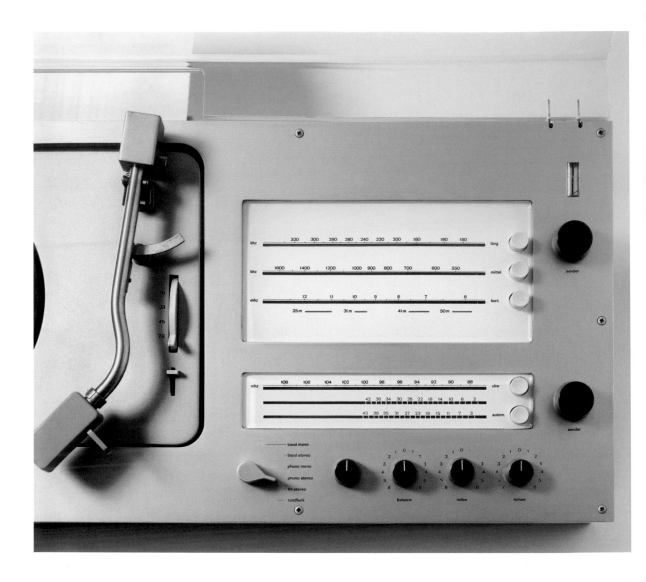

Braun "Audio 1" record player,
designed by **Dieter Rams**, 1962
(top: detail)

Braun hair dryer, designed by
Reinhold Weiss, 1964

Braun desk fan, designed by
Reinhold Weiss, 1961

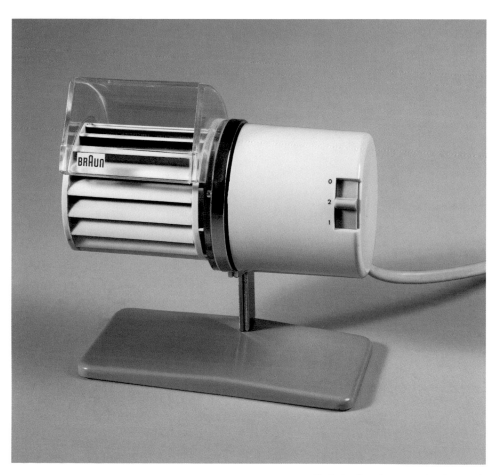

Plastic service, designed by **Massimo and Lella Vignelli**, 1964, produced from 1967 by Heller. The design won a Compasso d'Oro and was exhibited at the Museum of Modern Art in 1966

PAGE **43**
Chair, designed by **Verner Panton**, 1960, produced from 1967 by Herman Miller. The first single unit injection-moulded chair, fibreglass and polyester

Stacking ashtrays, designed by **Walter Zeischegg**, plastic, 1967

Stelton "Cylinda" service,
designed by **Arne Jacobsen**,
stainless steel, 1967
(bottom: icecube holder and
ashtray)

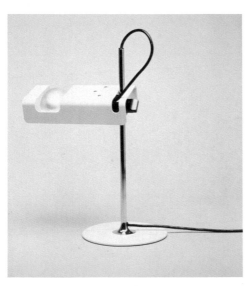

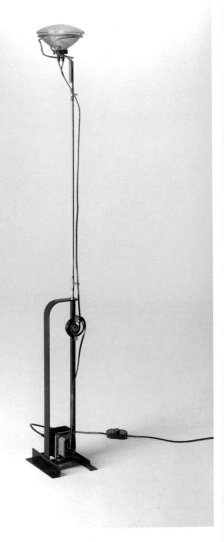

TOP
Flos "Arco" floor lamp,
designed by **Achille and Pier
Giacomo Castiglioni**, 1962

BOTTOM RIGHT
Flos "Toio" floor lamp,
designed by **Achille and Pier
Giacomo Castiglioni**, 1962

PAGE **47**
Living-room of Joe Colombo's
apartment in Milan, designed
in 1963

O-Luce "Spider" desk lamp,
designed by **Joe Colombo**,
1966

Toshiba poster, designed by
the **Nippon Design Centre**,
Tokyo, artist: Norio Ishiguro;
art director: Yoshio Suzuki,
c. 1966

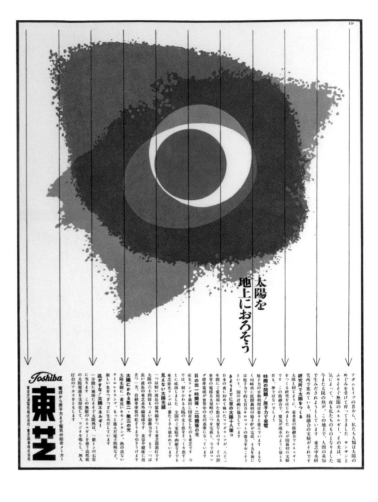

Honda car S 500, 1962

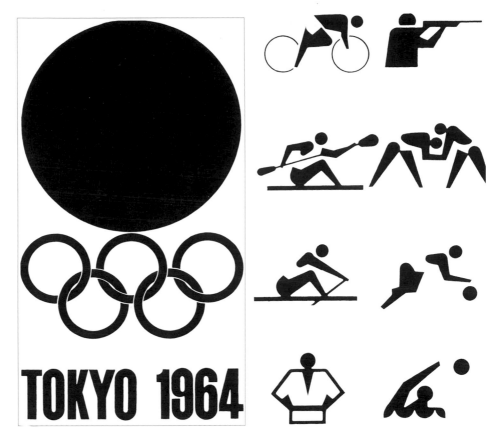

Nikon "F" single-lens reflex
camera, 1968

TOP
Airport lounge, Lima, Peru,
incorporating Artifort "042"
chair designed by **Geoffrey D.
Harcourt**, advertisement published 1967

BOTTOM
Signage for Schipol Airport,
Amsterdam, designed by **Total
Design**, 1967

PAGE **51**
Dulles airport passenger hall,
incorporating Herman Miller
"Tandem" seating, designed
by **Charles Eames**, 1962

52/53
passenger hall TWA,
New York, designed
arinen, 1962

ionalists – International Modernism

The Sixties witnessed major shifts and reappraisals of values in many areas of life. These changes had a profound impact on design and on attitudes to our man-made environments. The very notion of an Establishment provided a welcome target to the newly franchised, the urban young, the new affluent middle classes and the ambitious working classes of countries enjoying expanding economies. There was no longer room for the paternalistic tradition of taste dictated by the few privileged by class and education; large segments of the population wanted instant visual gratification, novelty, change, disposability. The new style-setters created a visual sensibility which is usually termed "Pop".

British Pop artist Richard Hamilton had defined the ingredients of this new aesthetic as "popular, transient, expendable, low-cost, mass-produced, young, witty, sexy, glamorous and Big Business". Popular culture provided the source material for Pop artists, who focused on the vitality of a certain visual vernacular of mass-produced objects; naive comic, packaging and advertising art; the vulgar debris of city streets; and the crass but seductive glamour of film, pop music and television. The visual feast which so intrigued the Pop artists grew out of the popular market place and popular media. It was essentially an innocent vernacular, its creators for the most part uncelebrated commercial artists.

Pop Art was an idiom of both fascination and irony. Significantly, it entered into a dialogue with popular culture; Pop generated energy in the exchanges between "High" art and "Low" art. fine and commercial artists fuelled one another and many designers tapped deliberately into the rich vein of this overlap in search of colours, motifs and, above all, attitude. It is symptomatic of the fluid nature of this dialogue that Andy Warhol, Pop's most celebrated exponent, had started as a commercial illustrator and store-window designer; James Rosenquist had been a billboard painter. Mario Amaya asked, in his pioneering 1965 survey *Pop Art*, whether "commercial packaging reminds us of [Richard] Smith's work, or whether his work reminds us of commercial packaging?". Smith's answer confirmed that "The give and take between the two is so enmeshed that I don't know which is foremost".

Pop design devised its own rules, the antithesis of Modernist ideology, yet not antagonistic to Modernism. Pop was about being modern in a different though not exclusive sense, the modern of fashionable high-impact design; a never-mind-about-tomorrow, brash, superficial modern; the modern of billboards and supermarkets; modern in the sense of being a part of a collective wish-fulfilment fantasy of up-to-the-minute consumer gadgetry, packaging, advertising and fashion. Pop design was integral to the so-called

In den sechziger Jahren vollzogen sich in vielen Lebensbereichen einschneidende Veränderungen, die mit Neuorientierungen in den Wertevorstellungen einhergingen. Diese Umwälzungen hatten natürlich auch nachhaltige Auswirkungen auf das Design und die Einstellung gegenüber der von den Menschen geschaffenen Umwelt. Vor allem in Ländern mit starkem wirtschaftlichen Aufschwung wurde der Begriff »Establishment« für die Jugendlichen, die jungen Großstadtbewohner, die zunehmend wohlhabenden Mittelständler und die ehrgeizige Arbeiterschicht zu einer Zielscheibe des Widerstandes. Das von den Vätern ererbte Traditionsbewußtsein in bezug auf den Geschmack, der von einigen wenigen der privilegierten Klasse diktiert und durch Erziehung weitergegeben worden war, hatte sich überlebt.

Große Teile der Bevölkerung wollten nun an einem unmittelbaren visuellen Genuß, am Reiz des Neuen und der Abwechslung, an der Verfügbarkeit der vielfältigen Dinge teilhaben. Die Vorreiter des neuen Stils kreierten eine visuelle Sinnlichkeit, die sehr bald mit dem Begriff »Pop« ettiketiert wurde.

Der britische Pop-Künstler Richard Hamilton benannte die wesentlichen Merkmale dieser neuen Ästhetik als »populär, vergänglich, entbehrlich, preisgünstig, massenproduziert, jugendlich, witzig, sexy, glamourös und als Big Business«. Die Alltagskultur lieferte den Pop-Künstlern ihre Anregungen, denn sie konzentrierten sich in ihrer Arbeit ganz auf die vitale Aussagekraft eines optischen Angebots, wie es Massenprodukte, naive Comics, Werbung, Verpackung und sogar der ganz normale Abfall der Großstadtstraßen in Hülle und Fülle lieferten; nicht zu vergessen der vordergründige und doch so verführerische Glanz der Kinofilme, der Unterhaltungsmusik und des Fernsehens. Alle diese optischen Reize, von denen die Pop-Künstler so sehr fasziniert wurden, waren ein Produkt der Konsumgesellschaft und der Massenmedien. Im Grunde war es also ein unschuldiges Idiom, ein optisches Verständigungsmittel, das von namentlich kaum bekannten Kommerzkünstlern geprägt wurde.

Pop Art stand für Faszination und Ironie. Bezeichnenderweise trat sie in Dialog mit der Alltagskultur und setzte Energien für den Austausch zwischen »hoher« und »niederer« Kunst frei. Künstler und Gebrauchsgrafiker, regten sich gegenseitig an, und viele Gestalter schöpften bei ihrer Suche nach Farben, Motiven und vor allem nach einer weltanschaulichen Position bewußt aus diesem Zusammenstrom von Ideen. Symptomatisch für das Fließende, das Grenzüberschreitende dieses Dialogs ist sicherlich das Beispiel Andy Warhols, des meistgefeierten Exponenten der Pop Art, der seine Karriere als Werbegrafiker und Schaufensterdekorateur begonnen hatte. Ähnlich James Rosenquist, der ursprünglich Plakatmaler gewesen war. Mario Amaya stellte 1965 in seiner wegweisenden Abhandlung »Pop Art« die bezeichnende Frage, ob »kommerzielle Verpackungen uns an [Richard]

Les années soixante virent bien des changements et bien des remises en question dans de nombreux domaines et l'impact sur le design et la façon de percevoir son environnement en fut important. La notion même d'un «Establishment» devint la cible favorite de ces nouveaux affranchis des pays à forte croissance économique: jeunes des villes, nouvelles classes moyennes aisées et classes ouvrières pleines d'ambition. Il n'y avait plus de place pour la tradition paternaliste du bon goût tel que l'imposaient quelques privilégiés; une grande partie de la population réclamait une gratification visuelle immédiate, de la nouveauté, du changement, du provisoire. Le ton était donné pour que naisse cette sensibilité visuelle qu'on a coutume de qualifier de «pop».

L'artiste pop anglais Richard Hamilton a pu dire que les ingrédients de cette esthétique nouvelle étaient «le populaire, le provisoire, le transformable, le bon marché, le produit de série, le jeune, le drôle, le ‹sexy›, le brillant et le ‹Big Business›.» La culture populaire devint le matériau d'inspiration des artistes pop qui s'intéressaient à l'«argot visuel», plein de vitalité, aux produits d'usage courant, aux bandes dessinées, à l'art de la publicité, aux banalités criardes du conditionnement et des rues et au clinquant des films, de la musique pop et de la télévision. L'orgie visuelle qui intriguait tant les artistes pop naissait de la rue et des médias populaires. C'était essentiellement un idiome naïf dont les inventeurs étaient pour la plupart d'obscurs artistes commerciaux.

L'art pop exprimait à la fois la fascination et l'ironie. Son dialogue avec la culture populaire est significatif; c'est dans l'énergie dégagée par les échanges entre l'art dit «noble» et l'art sans majuscule, dans ce riche filon produit de l'interaction entre artistes «purs» et artistes «commerciaux», que les designers cherchèrent leurs couleurs, leurs thèmes et, surtout, leurs attitudes. Parfaite illustration de la liberté de ce dialogue, le cas de Andy Warhol, qui avait commencé comme illustrateur publicitaire et étalagiste, et celui de James Rosenquist, affichiste. Dans une des premières études sur le sujet, «Pop Art», écrite en 1965, Mario Amaya se demande si «le conditionnement publicitaire évoque l'œuvre de [Richard] Smith ou si l'œuvre de cet artiste évoque le conditionnement publicitaire». La réponse de Smith: «Les rapports entre les deux sont si étroits que je ne sais pas ce qui prédomine.»

Le design pop dicta sa propre loi, antithèse de l'idéologie moderniste mais non opposée à elle. Le style pop consistait à être moderne d'une façon différente mais non exclusive, d'une modernité accessible à tous, d'une modernité désinvolte, frimeuse, superficielle, qui se placardait sur les murs et dans les supermarchés, et qui donnait le sentiment de faire partie d'un fantasme collectif, fait de gadgets, de conditionnements bigarrés, de «pub» et de mode. Le design pop faisait partie intégrante du «American Dream», conception matérialiste

Pop Culture – Pop Style

Pop-Kultur – Pop-Stil

La Culture Pop – Le Style Pop

American Dream, an all-consuming philosophy of materialism which, in the early Sixties, ruled untarnished over the West. Even Modernist designs could become subsumed into this Dream. It was Richard Hamilton who, with consummate irony, incorporated Braun electrical goods in his paintings, transforming Modernist icons into Pop symbols. He had paid his respects in another, earlier work, *Hommage à Chrysler Corp.* (1957), to that enduring Pop icon, the American motor car. Pop's appetite was voracious and catholic. Not without reason did author Christopher Booker entitle his study of Britain in the Sixties *The Neophiliacs*.

Pop culture drew on myriad sources as well as creating its own instant heroes and iconography. Peter Blake's 1967 cover for the Beatles' *Sgt. Pepper's Lonely Hearts Club Band* album is an instant lexicon of Pop heroes and heroines. Naive fairground art, pin-ups, archery targets, flags, particularly of course the stars and stripes and the Union Jack, were identified by artists as subject matter for their art and were at the same time reinterpreted by designers within the dictates of their commercial work. The result was a cycle of homage, plunder and appropriation. Tom Wesselmann's *Great American Nudes* incorporated actual consumer goods, like the telephone which was made to ring during an opening; Allen Jones made sculptures of exaggerated centrefold/fetish catalogue nudes which doubled as furniture, aggressively challenging the fine art versus functional design divide; Roy Lichtenstein's stylised recycled 1930 graphics were used as a paper design and on ceramic tableware. Jasper Johns painted the American flag and targets and cast two beer cans in bronze; commercial artists used flags and bright coloured targets on book jackets, boxes, alarm clocks, tea towels and record sleeves. A major review of American Pop Art at the Venice Biennale in 1964 gave extra impetus to the interaction.

Through the Sixties, influences from the fine arts on design were wide-ranging and embraced many modes beyond pure Pop itself, though Pop was crucial in opening this discourse. Of central importance was the immediate impact on design of the work of the second generation of American abstractionists. They rejected the emotionally charged painterliness of the Abstract Expressionists in favour of a cool, graphic approach to form and colour. These artists, certain of whom were categorized as Hard Edge and Colour Field Abstractionists, worked in flat areas of strong colour, usually on a heroic, mural scale. Their work often has an impersonal feel in its execution; they eschewed the impassioned brush strokes of Pollock and his contemporaries, favouring smooth, flat application, sometimes soaking the paint into unprimed canvas. What designers, particularly those working in two-dimensional media, found so exciting about the canvases of

Smiths Arbeiten erinnern, oder uns seine Arbeit an kommerzielle Verpackungen erinnern?« Smiths Antwort bestätigte, daß »das Geben und Nehmen zwischen beiden derart ineinandergreift, daß ich nicht weiß, was zuerst kommt«.

Das Pop-Design entwickelte seine eigenen Gesetzmäßigkeit, die zwar einen Gegenentwurf zur modernistischen Ideologie darstellten, dabei aber nicht im Widerspruch zum Modernismus standen. Pop bedeutete, in einem anderen, nicht ausschließlichen Sinne modern zu sein: im Sinne von modisch und hochgradig zeitgemäß. Eine oberflächliche, knallige, völlig unbekümmerte Modernität, wie sie auf Werbeplakaten und in Supermärkten zu sehen war; eine Modernität im Sinne einer kollektiven Phantasie, die ganz auf Wunscherfüllung ausgerichtet war. Diese Wunschphantasie beinhaltete ein Konsumverhalten, das in bezug auf technische Geräte, Verpackung, Werbung und Mode immer den allerneuesten Stand verlangte.

Pop-Design war untrennbar verbunden mit dem amerikanischen Traum, einer absolut konsumierenden Weltanschauung von unverhohlenem Materialismus, die in den frühen sechziger Jahren die gesamte westliche Welt beherrschte. Selbst modernistische Entwürfe ließen sich in diesen Traum einbauen. Richard Hamilton führte es mit vollendeter Ironie vor, indem er Braun-Elektrogeräte in seine Gemälde einarbeitete und damit modernistische Ikonen zu Pop-Symbolen erhob. Schon in einem früheren Werk, *Hommage à Chrysler Corp.* von 1957, hatte er der ewigen Pop-Ikone, dem amerikanischen Automobil, seine Referenz erwiesen. Der Appetit von Pop war unersättlich und allumfassend. Nicht ohne Grund gab der Autor Christopher Booker seiner Studie über das Großbritannien der sechziger Jahre den Titel »The Neophiliacs« (»Besessen von der Liebe zum Neuen«).

Die Pop-Kultur schöpfte nicht nur aus zahllosen Quellen, sie schuf sich auch ihre Augenblickshelden und ihre Augenblicks-Ikonographie. Das von Peter Blake 1967 gestaltete Cover für das Plattenalbum der Beatles »Sgt. Pepper's Lonely Hearts Club Band« gleicht einem »Instant-Lexikon« der Pop-Heldinnen und -Helden. Naive Jahrmarktskulissen, Pin-up-Figuren, Zielscheiben, Flaggen, vor allem natürlich das amerikanische Sternenbanner (Stars and Stripes) und der britische Union Jack wurden für die Künstler zu Bildgegenständen und zum Thema ihrer Kunst. Zugleich wurden sie von Designern rückinterpretiert, die diese Gegenstände wiederum dem Diktat ihrer kommerziellen Arbeit unterwarfen. So entstand ein Kreislauf von Hommage, Plünderung und Aneignung.

Tom Wesselmann arbeitete in seine *Great American Nudes* gängige Konsumgüter ein, zum Beispiel ein Telefon, das man während einer Vernissage klingeln ließ. Allen Jones schuf lebensgroße Skulpturen von Pin-up-Schönheiten wie aus Fetisch-Katalogen, die zugleich als

Andy Warhol: "Campbell's Soup Can", silk screen and acrylic on canvas, 1965

de la vie qui, au début des années soixante, régnait en maître en Occident. Le design moderniste lui-même a parfois subi l'emprise de ce «rêve». On a vu Richard Hamilton incorporer, avec une ironie consommée, des produits Braun dans ses toiles, transformant ainsi des icônes modernistes en symboles pop. Dans une œuvre plus ancienne, *Hommage à Chrysler Corp.* (1957), il avait payé tribut à cette image récurrente du pop art, l'automobile américaine. L'appétit de la génération pop était dévorant et universel. Christopher Booker choisit non sans raison de titrer son étude de l'Angleterre des années soixante «The Neophiliacs».

La culture pop s'abreuva à de nombreuses sources mais elle créa aussi ses héros d'un jour et son iconographie. La jaquette de l'album des Beatles «Sgt. Pepper's Lonely Hearts Club Band» (1967) de Peter Blake est un sommaire de tous ces héros et héroïnes. Kermesses naïves, pin-ups, cibles, drapeaux, surtout anglais et américains, furent reconnus par les artistes de l'époque qui réinterprétaient à loisir les illustrateurs commerciaux. D'où l'existence d'un cycle de références, de pillages, d'appropriations. La série des *Great American Nudes* de Tom Wesselmann faisait intervenir des accessoires quotidiens, un téléphone, par exemple, qu'on fit sonner lors d'un vernissage. Allen Jones créa à partir de pin-ups des sculptures nues qui étaient aussi des meubles, renvoyant dos à dos l'Art avec un grand A et le design fonctionnel. Les projets graphiques de Roy Lichtenstein qui s'inspirait du style 1930 furent édités sur papier et sur des services en céramique. Jasper Johns peignit le drapeau américain ainsi que des cibles et fondit en bronze deux boîtes de bière. Des illustrateurs commerciaux reproduisirent le motif des drapeaux et des cibles sur des jaquettes de livres et de disques, sur des boîtes, des réveils, des torchons. Une importante exposition du Pop Art américain, à la Biennale de Venise de 1964, encouragea par ailleurs cette interaction.

Tout au long des années soixante, l'influence de l'art sur le design s'est manifestée bien au-delà des limites du pop. Il n'en demeure pas moins que le style pop eut un rôle prépondérant dans l'ouverture du dialogue. La deuxième génération d'artistes à style abstrait américains eut une forte influence sur le design. Rejetant l'élément émotionnel de l'expressionnisme abstrait, cette école de peinture choisit une approche détachée, toute graphique, de la forme et de la couleur. Ces artistes, dont certains ont été catalogués comme faisant partie du «hard edge» ou du «colour field», peignaient en plans de couleurs fortes, généralement sur une échelle monumentale. Il se dégage souvent de leur œuvre quelque chose d'impersonnel; ils cherchaient à prendre leurs distances du coup de pinceau passionné de Pollock et de ses contemporains pour une planéité obtenue parfois en appliquant la couleur sur une toile sans apprêt. Ce que les designers, surtout ceux qui travaillaient en deux dimensions, trouvaient si stimulant dans les toiles

Richard Hamilton: "Still Life", coloured photograph on wood, 1965

Ellsworth Kelly, Morris Louis, Kenneth Noland and Frank Stella were those bold graphic statements and the drama of strong primary colours and vibrant contrasts. It was love at first sight as commercial artists were first exposed to the new language of abstract art.

The result was a boldness with saturated primaries and other strong colours which came to be associated with the period. This was evidenced in graphic and in product design, particularly when the new palette was allied to the technologies of injection-moulded plastics. Italian manufacturers such as Kartell, Danese and Artemide used reds, yellows, greens, oranges which could have been appropriated from Colour Field canvases. Stella-inspired stripes found their way into an Olivetti advertisement, Robert Indiana's *Love* painting was adapted as a poster by Neiman Marcus, Ellsworth Kelly's bold canvases, with their flat areas of colour and play between "negative" and "positive" space inspired graphic design equivalents in myriad contexts.

Central to the endeavours of many artists in the early Sixties was the challenge of creating an art of audience involvement. They wanted to break the distance between artifact and audience. The spectator was to be drawn in as active participant. As the spectator moved, so the work of art would change. The means used were three-dimensional in constructions which the audience was obliged to walk through; or created an illusion of a third dimension through optical tricks or the play of lights. "Situation", "Op" and "Kinetic" art were the end product. And the by-products were immediately evident in the market place.

The Situation Art of the early Sixties challenged conventional easel painting and made the three-dimensional work into a kind of event. The boundary became blurred between the ambitions of artists creating these works that existed and demanded to be experienced in three dimensions, and designers and decorators creating "environments", their domestic equivalents. These took the form of dramatic, all-enveloping colour schemes or such features as conversation pits or womb-like group seating units.

The impact of Bridget Riley's visually disturbing "Op" canvases, which first achieved wide recognition in 1964/65, was instant and dramatic. The dazzling, eye-catching visual effects of "Op" which she pioneered proved enormously useful to designers of logos, advertising graphics, fabrics and seemingly any two-dimensional surface which sought high impact in a fashionable idiom. These dramatic black and white patterns became ubiquitous. In France artist Victor Vasarely pursued comparable effects in colour and broadened the repertoire of "Op", and his works in turn became grist to the mill of fashionable two-dimensional design. The shifting optical patterns of commercial neon signage, integrated into Pop as a

Möbelstücke dienten und damit die Grenze zwischen Kunst und funktionellem Design aggressiv in Frage stellten. Roy Lichtensteins stilisierte Aufbereitungen von Grafiken aus den dreißiger Jahren wurden als Tapetenmuster und als Dekore auf Keramikgeschirren verwendet. Jasper Johns malte die amerikanische Flagge und Zielscheiben, desweiteren goß er zwei Bierdosen in Bronze. Gebrauchsgrafiker verwendeten dieselben Motive, Flaggen und leuchtendbunte Zielscheiben, zur Gestaltung und Dekoration von Buchumschlägen, Schachteln und Büchsen, Weckern, Geschirrtüchern und Plattenhüllen. Eine umfassende Werkschau der amerikanischen Pop Art auf der Biennale in Venedig im Jahre 1964 gab eine Fülle von Anregungen für den Ideenaustausch, für die wechselseitige Inspiration.

In den sechziger Jahren gingen von der bildenden Kunst vielfältige und weitreichende Einflüsse auf das Design aus. Sie kamen aus ganz unterschiedlichen Stilrichtungen, die sich nicht nur auf die reine Pop Art beschränkten, wenngleich diese bei der Eröffnung dieses Dialogs tonangebend war. Eine zentrale Bedeutung nimmt dabei die zweite Generation amerikanischer abstrakter Künstler ein, deren Werke unmittelbare Wirkung auf das Design ausübten. Sie verwarfen die emotionsgeladene gestische Malerei der abstrakten Expressionisten zugunsten eines kühlen, grafischen Umgangs mit Form und Farbe.

Diese Künstler, deren Werke als Hard Edge und Farbfeldmalerei kategorisiert wurden, arbeiteten großflächig mit starken Farben und bevorzugten Formate von heroischen Dimensionen. Ihre Arbeiten wirkten häufig aufgrund der glatten Maltechnik recht unpersönlich. Sie vermieden die leidenschaftlich gestischen Pinselstriche eines Jackson Pollock und seiner Zeitgenossen und bevorzugten einen flachen, großflächigen Farbauftrag. Bisweilen ließen sie die Farbe einfach in die nicht grundierte Leinwand einsickern. Designer, vor allem jene, die mit zweidimensionalen Medien arbeiteten, waren von den Bildern von Ellsworth Kelly, Morris Louis, Kenneth Noland und Frank Stella begeistert. Für ihre eigene Arbeit fanden sie die kühnen grafischen Anlagen der Gemälde, die drastischen Effekte der Primärfarben und die vibrierenden Kontraste höchst anregend. Es war Liebe auf den ersten Blick, die die Gebrauchskünstler bei der Begegnung mit einer neuen Farb- und Formensprache der abstrakten Kunst bekundeten.

Der unerschrockene Umgang mit satten Primärfarben und anderen starken oder grellen Farben sollte für diese Epoche charakteristisch werden. Dies zeigte sich sehr bald auch in der Gebrauchsgrafik und im Produktdesign, vor allem bei der Anwendung der neuen Farbpalette auf Kunststoffobjekten, die im Spritzgußverfahren hergestellt wurden. Italienische Hersteller wie Kartell, Danese und Artemide verwendeten Rot-, Gelb-, Grün- und Orangetöne, die Werken der Farbfeldmalerei hätten entnommen sein können. In Farbstreifen gegliederte Flächen,

Printed paper, designed by
Roy Lichtenstein, c. 1965

d'Ellsworth Kelly, de Morris Louis, de Kenneth Noland et de Frank Stella, c'était ces puissantes constructions graphiques, la force de ces couleurs primaires et ces vibrants contrastes. Entre les artistes commerciaux et le langage nouveau de l'art abstrait ce fut le coup de foudre.

Le résultat en fut un style plein de hardiesse utilisant des couleurs primaires saturées et d'autres couleurs fortes, qui pour nous sont inséparables de cette époque. Son domaine fut celui du design graphique et du design de produits, surtout lorsque cette nouvelle palette put s'exprimer par la technique du plastique moulé par injection. Des fabricants italiens tels que Kartell, Danese et Artemide produisirent des rouges, des jaunes, des verts et des orange qui semblaient venir tout droit des toiles de l'abstraction géométrique. Des rayures à la Stella se retrouvèrent dans une publicité pour Olivetti. Le tableau de Robert Indiana, *Love*, fut adapté pour une affiche par Neiman Marcus, les belles toiles d'Ellsworth Kelly, avec leurs plans chromatiques et le jeu créé entre ses espaces «négatifs» et «positifs» furent une source d'inspiration pour des myriades de réalisations graphiques.

Une chose était chère au cœur de bien des artistes, au début des années soixante: parvenir à impliquer le public dans le processus de création, à abolir la distance qui le séparait de l'œuvre, à faire de lui un participant à part entière. Il fallait que si le spectateur bouge, l'œuvre change. Pour ce faire on réalisa des constructions tridimensionnelles au travers desquelles on pouvait passer ou des œuvres qui donnaient l'illusion de la profondeur par des ruses optiques ou des jeux de lumière. C'est ainsi que l'on arriva au situationnisme, à l'op art et à l'art kinétique. Avec, aussitôt, leurs retombées commerciales.

L'art situationniste du début de la décennie remettait en question les conventions de la peinture traditionnelle et faisait de l'œuvre en trois dimensions une sorte de «happening». La frontière entre ces artistes dont l'œuvre exigeait d'être visualisée en trois dimensions et les designers et décorateurs devenait de plus en plus floue. Ceux-ci créaient des environnements, équivalents domestiques de l'art situationniste, dont les combinaisons de couleurs étaient destinées à générer telle ou telle ambiance, des modules du type «salon-fosse» ou des groupes de sièges en forme de matrice.

Le choc créé par les étonnantes toiles op art de Bridget Riley, qui furent reconnues du grand public dans les années 64–65, fut violent et immédiat. Les effets hallucinants de l'op art, dont elle fut la première représentante, allaient devenir extrêmement utiles aux designers de logos, de graphismes publicitaires, de tissus et, semble-t-il, de toute surface bi-dimensionnelle censée être «à la mode». Ces motifs dramatiques en noir et blanc se retrouvèrent partout. En France, Victor Vasarely poursuivit la même recherche, mais avec la couleur, élargissant ainsi le répertoire de l'op art, et, à leur tour, ses œuvres

Allen Jones: "Table, Chair and Hatstand", furniture modelled as female figures, 1969

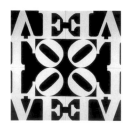

Robert Indiana: "Love Rising", acrylic on canvas, 1968

prime source, were as swiftly recycled into "Kinetic" light art and back into the repertoire of graphic design. Robert Brownjohn's credit sequence for the film *From Russia with Love* (1963) had defined a genre of commercial living light sculpture. "Op" and "Kinetic" art became a design source book of illusionistic effects exploiting pattern, shimmering colour contrast and the play of light. The Introduction to *Decorative Art in Modern Interiors 1968–69* encouraged the experimental synthesis of "art and architecture, furniture and art, light, colour and electronics", a rallying call to a multimedia exploration for the electronic age.

The Sixties saw the revival of interest in the decorative arts of the turn of the century. Major retrospectives in London and Paris of the work of Alphonse Mucha (1963 and 1966) and at the Victoria and Albert Museum, London, of the drawings of Aubrey Beardsley (1966) heralded the entry into the iconography of popular culture of the work of these masters of line. Their work and other features of the Art Nouveau style also became frequent ingredients in the pot pourri of sources, including "Op" and "Pop" references, which came together in 1967 in the phenomenon of Psychedelic art. Born simultaneously in the drug and music related sub-cultures of San Francisco and London, psychedelia emerged as one of the most forceful expressions of the Sixties. The style, rich in colour, reference and effect, suggested the liberation of the imagination in complex graphics which hovered on the limits of legibility.

Wes Wilson was the foremost San Francisco protagonist of this mode. Much of his work was made as promotional graphics for two concert venues, the Avalon Ballroom and the Fillmore Auditorium. His most able British counterpart was the team of Michael English and Nigel Waymouth, designing under the name of Hapshash and the Coloured Coat. For a brief period of a year or two they produced posters, album covers and other graphics in a style which marked a distinct shift in the Sixties mood, away from the innocent optimism of the earlier years of the decade. American Pop-Psychedelic artist Peter Max and the Dutch artists The Fool, sponsored by the Beatles' Apple company, decorated every available surface, in every medium, with a riot of psychedelic colour and pattern and neo-surrealistic motif. The work of these artists was an escape into fantasy, the end of a more innocent dream.

die von Bildern Frank Stellas inspiriert waren, fanden sich in einer Olivetti-Reklame wieder. Robert Indianas Gemälde *Love* diente Neiman Marcus als Vorlage für ein Poster, Ellsworth Kellys minimalistische Bilder mit ihren planen Farbfeldern und ihrem optischen Spiel des Figur-Grund-Austauschs, hier dem Wechselspiel von positiven und negativen Flächen, inspirierten nicht nur die Werbegrafik, sondern alle grafischen Bereiche.

Viele Künstler der frühen sechziger Jahre formulierten als zentrales Anliegen ihrer Arbeit eine Beteiligung des Publikums an ihrer Kunst: Sie wollten die Distanz zwischen Kunstwerk und Publikum aufheben, den Betrachter als aktiven Teilnehmer in das Werk einbeziehen. Bewegte sich der Betrachter, sollte sich das Kunstwerk ebenfalls verändern. Als geeignetes Mittel sahen die Künstler die Schaffung dreidimensionaler Konstruktionen an, die das Publikum zu begehen oder zu durchwandern hatte. Oder aber es wurde durch optische Tricks und Lichteffekte die Illusion einer dritten Dimension erzeugt. So entstanden als neue Richtungen Situation Art, Op Art und Kinetische Kunst. Und unverzüglich machten sich auf dem Markt die Einflüsse auf die kommerzielle Gebrauchskunst bemerkbar.

Die Situation Art der frühen sechziger Jahre stellte das konventionelle Malen an der Staffelei in Frage und verlieh dem dreidimensionalen Werk Ereignischarakter. Schon bald wurden die Grenzen fließend zwischen den Ambitionen der bildenden Künstler und denen der Gebrauchskünstler. Beide wollten ihre Intentionen in dreidimensionalen Werken zum Ausdruck bringen, beider Produkte erforderten die Erfahrbarkeit in der Dreidimensionalität.

Designer und Innenausstatter schufen ebenso wie die bildenden Künstler Environments, jedoch als Gebrauchsgegenstände im Wohnbereich. Sie entwarfen Wohnlandschaften in spektakulären Farbkompositionen, die die gesamte Einrichtung umfaßten. Es entstanden höchst aussagekräftige Wohnelemente wie Konversationsbuchten oder schalenartige Sitzgruppen.

Die optisch verwirrenden Op Art-Gemälde, mit denen Bridget Riley 1964/65 kurzzeitig sehr erfolgreich war, lebten von ihrer unmittelbaren, fast überwältigenden Wirkung. Die ins Auge springenden, aufreizenden visuellen Effekte dieser Wegbereiterin der Op Art erwiesen sich als höchst geeignet für Designer von Logos, Signets, Werbegrafiken, Stoffen und allen zweidimensionalen Flächen, die einer aussagekräftigen Gestaltung in einer zeitgemäßen grafischen Sprache bedurften. Schon bald waren die spektakulären Schwarz-weiß-Muster überall zu sehen.

In Frankreich entwickelte der Künstler Victor Vasarely ähnliche Effekte mit Farben und erweiterte damit nicht nur das Ausdrucksspektrum der Op Art, sondern beeinflußte auch die Gestalter eines modischen zweidimensionalen Designs nachhaltig. Auch die beweglichen Motive von Neonreklamen oder die schnell wechselnden

alimentèrent le design «dans le vent». Les enseignes de néon qui avaient été une des inspirations du pop art se trouvèrent recyclées tout aussi rapidement dans l'art cinétique lumineux et réintégrées dans le domaine du design graphique. Pour le générique du film «Bons baisers de Russie» (1963), Robert Brownjohn créa une sculpture lumineuse vivante. L'op art et le cinétisme devinrent pour le design une sorte d'anthologie d'effets spéciaux basés sur le motif, le contraste vibratoire des couleurs et les jeux de lumière. Dans l'introduction du livre «Decorative Art in Modern Interiors 1968–69», on trouve un appel à la synthèse expérimentale de «l'art et de l'architecture, du mobilier et de l'art, de la lumière, de la couleur et de l'électronique», un cri de ralliement pour une recherche multi-médias à l'ère électronique.

Les années soixante connurent un regain d'intérêt pour les arts décoratifs de la fin du siècle. D'importantes rétrospectives à Londres et à Paris de l'œuvre d'Alphonse Mucha (en 1963 et en 1966) et, au Victoria and Albert Museum, à Londres, des dessins d'Aubrey Beardsley (en 1966) consacrèrent l'entrée de ces maîtres du trait dans l'iconographie de la culture populaire. Leurs œuvres et d'autres de style Art nouveau firent des apparitions fréquentes dans le pot-pourri des sources d'inspiration, en compagnie de références tirées de l'op art et du pop art qui s'amalgamèrent en 1967 pour former l'art psychédélique. Né simultanément des crypto-cultures de la drogue et de la musique à San Francisco et à Londres, l'art psychédélique devint l'un des modes d'expression les plus vivants des années soixante. Haut en couleur, plein de références et d'effets, ce style évoquait un imaginaire libéré en un graphisme complexe, à la limite de l'intelligible.

A San Francisco, le protagoniste du style psychédélique fut Wes Wilson. Une grande partie de son œuvre consista en travaux graphiques pour la promotion de deux salles de concert, l'Avalon Ballroom et le Fillmore Auditorium. En Angleterre, l'équipe de Michael English et Nigel Waymouth, sous le pseudonyme de Hapshash and the Coloured Coat, fut son équivalent le plus proche. Pendant une ou deux années, ils produisirent des affiches, des pochettes de disque et autres créations graphiques dans un style qui s'éloigne de l'optimisme naïf du début de la décennie. L'artiste pop et psychédélique américain Peter Max et les Hollandais The Fool, soutenus par les Beatles, décorèrent tout ce qui pouvait l'être, de toute façon possible, d'un flot de motifs et de couleurs psychédéliques et de thèmes néo-surréalistes. C'était là une fuite dans le fantasme et la fin d'un rêve innocent.

Poster for Neiman Marcus, designed by **Robert Indiana** with art director Ron Irebaugh, 1968

Biba art nouveau revival logo, designed by **John McConnell**, 1968

Bilder von kommerziellen Neonsignalen, die als eine wichtige Quelle in das Pop-Repertoire eingingen, tauchten als Ideengeber in der kinetischen Lichtkunst auf und kehrten modifiziert ebenso schnell zurück in die Formensprache der Gebrauchskunst. Robert Brownjohn konzipierte mit seinem Vorspann zu dem Film »Liebesgrüße aus Moskau« von 1963 ein neues kommerzielles Genre der lebenden Lichtskulptur. Op Art und Kinetische Kunst wurden gleichsam zum Musterbuch für illusionistische Effekte, die mit gleißenden Farbkontrasten, wirkungsvollen Mustern und Lichtspielen erzielt wurden. In der Einführung zu »Decorative Art in Modern Interiors 1968–69« wird eine Ermutigung zur experimentellen Synthese von »Kunst und Architektur, Möbeldesign und Kunst, Licht, Farbe und Elektronik« formuliert. Es ist ein Aufruf zu einem multimedialen Zusammenschluß, zu einer Durchdringung und gegenseitigen Befruchtung der Medien im elektronischen Zeitalter.

In den sechziger Jahren lebte auch das Interesse an der dekorativen Kunst der Jahrhundertwende wieder auf. Große Retrospektiven zum Werk von Alfons Mucha 1963 in London und 1966 in Paris sowie eine Ausstellung der Zeichnungen von Aubrey Beardsley 1966 im Victoria and Albert Museum in London bildeten den Auftakt für eine Rückbesinnung auf die Formensprache dieser Linienkünstler. Ihr Vokabular fand damit Eingang in die Ikonographie der Pop-Kultur.

Neben ihren Werken wurden auch andere charakteristische Ausdrucksformen von Jugendstil und Art Nouveau zu wesentlichen Bestandteilen eines Gemisches von Vorbildern und Quellen, zu denen natürlich auch Op Art und Pop-art gehörten, aus denen schließlich 1967 ein Phänomen erwuchs und sich speiste, das als psychedelische Kunst etikettiert wurde. »Psychedelia« war gleichzeitig in der von Drogen und Musik beherrschten Subkultur von San Francisco und London entstanden und erwies sich als eine der kraftvollsten und intensivsten Ausdrucksformen der sechziger Jahre. Der Stil war äußerst farbig, reich an Nuancen, Anspielungen und Effekten und suggerierte eine Befreiung der Phantasie, die sich in komplexen grafischen Gestaltungen Raum schuf; doch stießen diese Formulierungen häufig an die Grenzen der Lesbarkeit.

Wes Wilson war der Protagonist und herausragende Vertreter dieser Kunstrichtung. Ein Großteil seines Werkes bestand aus Werbeplakaten für zwei Konzertsäle, den Avalon Ballroom und das Fillmore Auditorium. Seine begabtesten Kollegen in Großbritannien, das Team von Michael English und Nigel Waymouth, signierten ihre Entwürfe mit dem Namen »Hapshash and the Coloured Coat«. In der kurzen Zeitspanne von kaum zwei Jahren produzierten sie Poster, Plattencover und andere Grafiken in einem Stil, an dem sich deutlich ein Stimmungsumschwung der späten sechziger Jahre ablesen ließ, denn er hob sich merklich von dem unschuldigen Optimismus der Frühphase dieses Jahrzehnts ab.

Der amerikanische Pop-Künstler der psychedelischen Richtung Peter Max und das niederländische Künstlerpaar »The Fool«, das von der Beatles-Firma Apple gesponsert wurde, dekorierten jede verfügbare Oberfläche, aus welchem Material und in welchem Medium auch immer, mit einer Orgie aus psychedelischen Farben, wuchernden Mustern und neosurrealistischen Motiven. In den Arbeiten dieser Künstler kam eine Flucht in die Phantasie zum Ausdruck, die das Ende eines eher unschuldigen Traums bezeichnete.

PAGE **63**
Psychedelic poster for a concert at the Avalon Ballroom, San Francisco, published by Family Dog Productions, 1967

TICKET OUTLETS – <u>SAN FRANCISCO:</u> MNASIDIKA (HAIGHT-ASHBURY), CITY LIGHTS BOOKS (NORTH BEACH), THE TOWN SQUIRE (1318 POLK). <u>BERKELEY:</u> DISCOUNT RECORDS. <u>SAUSALITO:</u> TIDE'S BOOKSTORE. <u>REDWOOD CITY:</u> REDWOOD HOUSE OF MUSIC (700 WINSLOW). <u>SAN MATEO:</u> TOWN & COUNTRY MUSIC CENTER (4TH & EL CAMINO). LA MER CAMERAS & MUSIC (HILLSDALE AT 19TH). <u>MENLO PARK:</u> KEPLER'S BOOKS & MAGAZINES (825 EL CAMINO). <u>SAN JOSE:</u> DISCORAMA (235 SO. FIRST ST).

No92-1   1967 © FAMILY DOG PRODUCTIONS 639 GOUGH ST., San Francisco, Calif. 94102

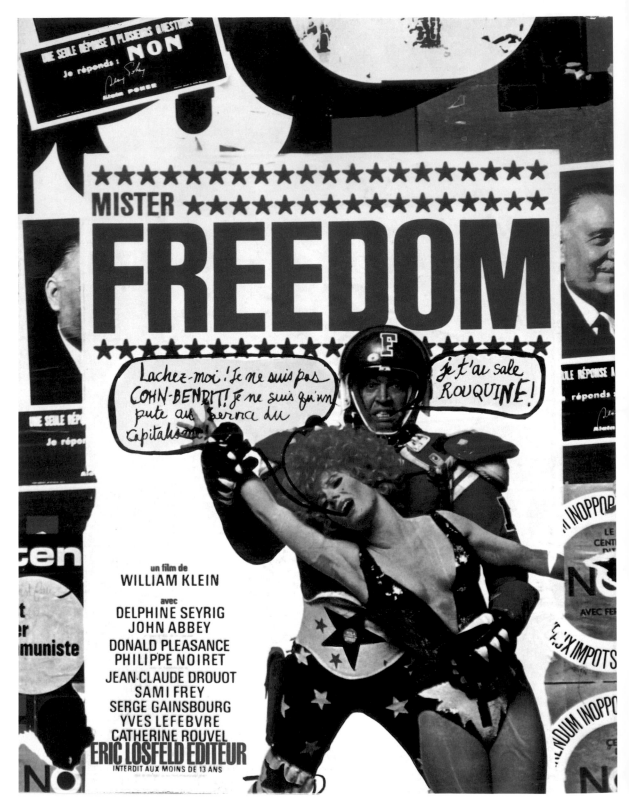

"Mr Freedom". Book cover incorporating the film poster, designed by **William Klein**, the film made 1967–68, the book published 1970

"Traces of Man", book cover, designed by **Herbert Spencer**, 1967

Safeway supermarket, Denver, Colorado, U.S.A., 1966

Tom Wesselmann: "Still Life 21", acrylic and collage on board with recorded tape of pouring drink, 1962

Sainsbury supermarket trolley full of packaged foods, mid-1960s

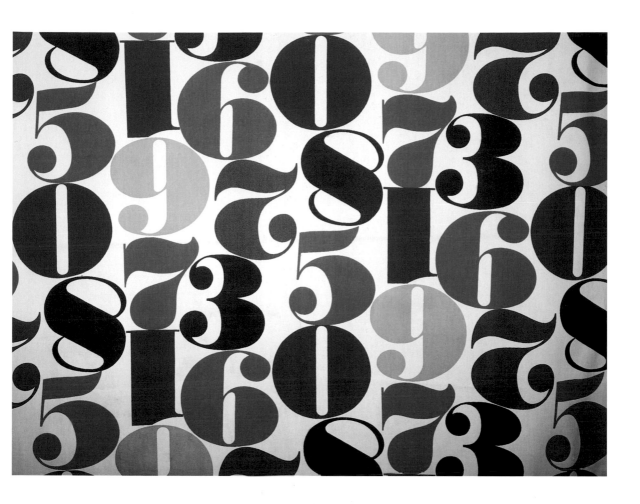

TOP
Textile design, c. 1965

BOTTOM
Promotional image for Habitat showing typical range of consumer goods, 1967

Pop objects by Dodo Designs, a company set up by Robin Farrow and Paula McGibbon, 1965 promotional photograph

Union Jack motif for a book jacket, designed by **Frederick Lambert**, 1967

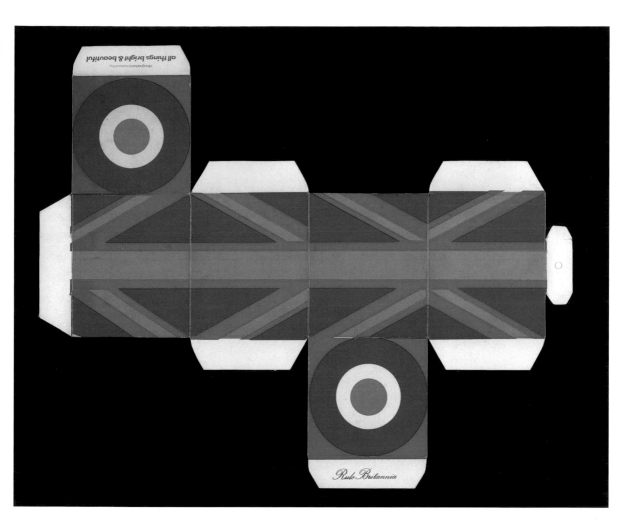

TOP
Box with stylised Union Jack
and target motifs, produced
by All Things Bright and
Beautiful, c. 1966–68

BOTTOM
Book jacket, designed by
Milton Glaser of Push Pin
Studios, early 1960s

Peter Blake: "Babe Rainbow", silk screen print on tin,
published by Dodo Designs, 1968

"Sgt. Pepper's Lonely Hearts Club Band", album cover, designed by **Peter Blake** and **Jann Haworth** with photographer Michael Cooper, 1967

Front-of-house still for the film "Blow Up", featuring "mini" dresses and a Dodo Designs head, 1966

"8 Painters", exhibition catalogue cover, Museum of Modern Art, Oxford 1968

Ellsworth Kelly: "Orange Blue 1",
oil on canvas, 1965

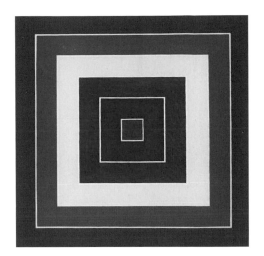

Frank Stella: "Palisades",
oil on canvas, 1962

Venini glass vase, designed by **Ludovico de Santillana**, produced
for Philips, the form derived from the shape of a T. V. screen,
1965

Cover of "Vogue", U.K.,
15 September 1965

Op Art motif from an advertisement for Pirelli Cinturato
tyres, c. 1966–67

TOP
Op Art still from the film "Qui êtes-vous Polly Maggoo?", designed by **William Klein**, 1966

BOTTOM
Hair style by Vidal Sassoon, 1965

TOP
Bridget Riley: "Fragments 5", silkscreen on plexiglass, 1965

BOTTOM LEFT
Op Art carpet, designed by **Antonio Boggeri** for Polymer
Montecatini Edison, Italy, c. 1966

BOTTOM RIGHT
Emblem of the International Wool Secretariat, designed by
Francesco Saroglia, c. 1965–66

PAGE **77**
Op Art advertisement for Danese, published 1967

MADE IN ITALY

DANESE

DIS. ENZO MARI

MILANO

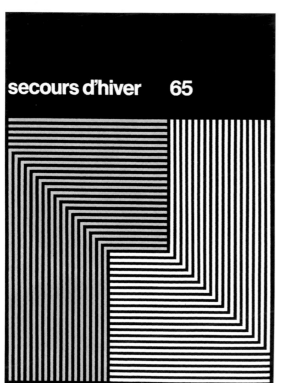

TOP
"Black and white" folding
chairs, designed by **Gae
Aulenti**, 1966, produced by
Centro Fly

LEFT
Op Art poster "Secours
d'Hiver", designed by **Jacques
Blanchard**, 1965

Logo for the 1968 Mexico
Olympics

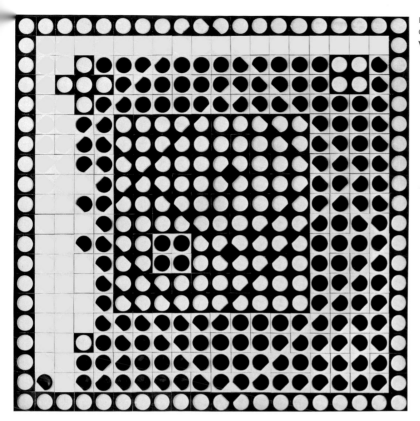

Rosenthal relief "NB 22 Caope", designed by **Victor Vasarely**, 1968

The Mexican pavilion at the Olympic games in Mexico 1968

Still from the credit sequence for the film "From Russia with Love", designed by **Robert Brownjohn**, 1963

Fashion picture by Norman Parkinson using double-exposure with New York street signage, for "Queen", 14 August 1963

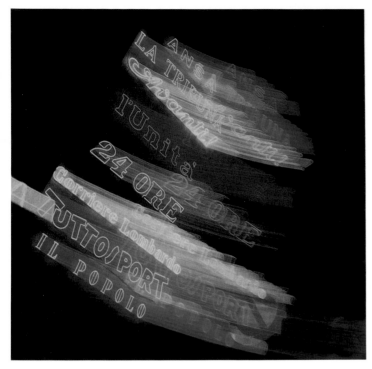

Neon typography for an advertisement, designed by **Rudolf Schucht** with photographer Forser-Heintzel, mid 1960s

Colour image from an advertisement for Ciba Dyes "In the cause of progress", designed by **Peter Stockli** and **Rolf Zubler** with art director Emil Hasler, mid 1960s

POWIĘKSZENIE

reżyseria
MICHELANGELO ANTONIONI

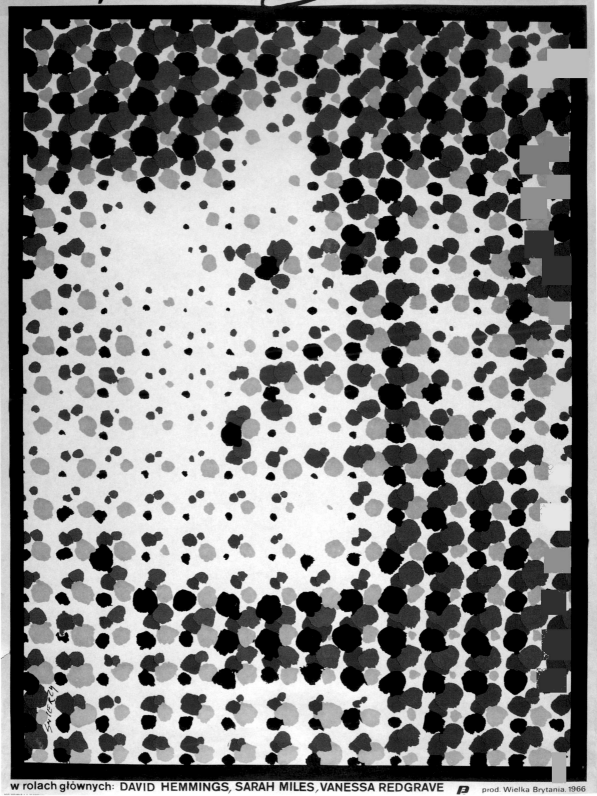

w rolach głównych: DAVID HEMMINGS, SARAH MILES, VANESSA REDGRAVE prod. Wielka Brytania. 1966

Concert flyer, designed by **Wes Wilson**, 1967

PAGE **82**
Poster for "Blow Up", Polish version, designed by **Waldemar Swierzy**, 1966

LEFT
Cover for "Oz" magazine,
designed by **Hapshash and
the Coloured Coat**, 1967

RIGHT
Art nouveau revival greetings
card, late 1960s

PAGE **85**
"Love" poster, designed by
Peter Max, c. 1967–68

Poster for The Who, designed
by **Hapshash and the
Coloured Coat**, published by
Osiris Visions Ltd, 1967

PAGE **87**
"A is for Apple" poster,
designed by **The Fool**,
c. 1967–68

20th CENTURY-FOX presents

THE ROLLING STONES in GIMME SHELTER A COLOUR BY DE LUXE

20th CENTURY-FOX presents

THE ROLLING STONES in GIMME SHELTER A COLOUR BY DE LUXE

Stills from the film "Gimme
Shelter", documenting the
Rolling Stones' Altamont con-
cert, December 1969

PAGE **88**
Concert flyer, designed by
Wes Wilson, 1967

Psychedelic landscape from the film "2001: A Space Odyssey" by Stanley Kubrick, 1968

Psychedelic/Surrealist landscape, designed by Simon and Marikje of **The Fool**, sold in the Beatles' retail outlet, Apple, opened December 1967

PAGE **91**
Room design at the "Visiona" exhibition by Bayer AG, designed by **Verner Panton**, 1968

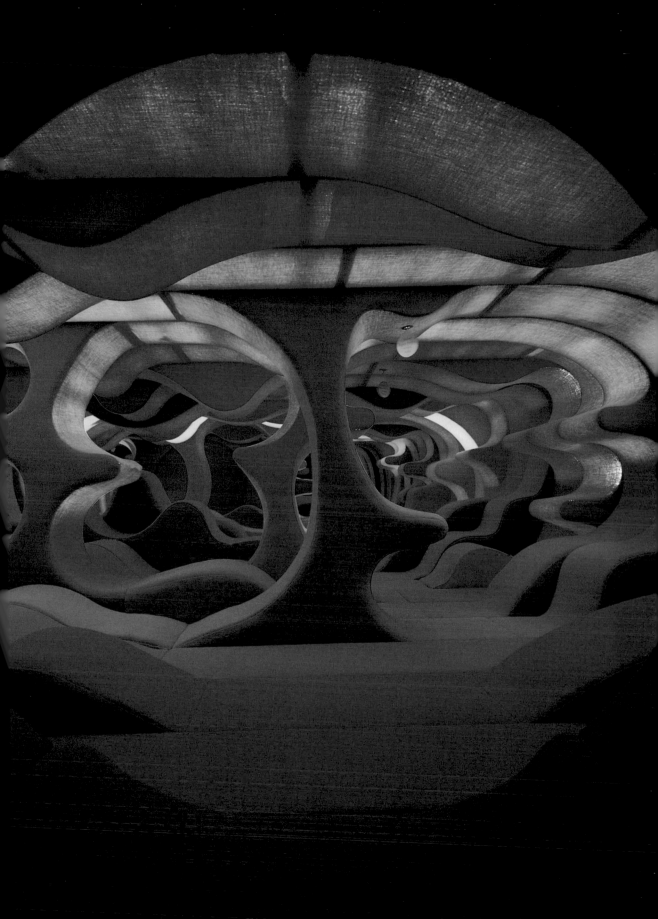

"Malitte" seating system,
designed by **Roberto Sebastian
Matta**, 1966

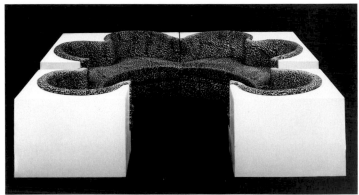

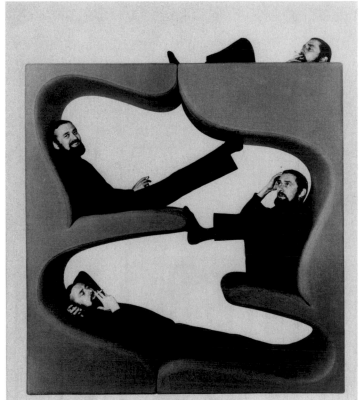

TOP
"Safari" seating system,
designed by **Archizoom**, 1967

BOTTOM
Verner Panton in modular
seating system "Living" tower,
multiple exposure photo-
graph, 1969

The Cold War provided the international political background to the Sixties. The American Dream of plenty was thrown into sharper relief by contrast with the standards of living in the Communist Eastern bloc. Implicit in the American promise was a correlation of political and market freedoms. The manufacturer and the consumer had become the motor of the state, the source of energy and wealth which defined the success of the nation. Moreover, the United States had achieved considerable momentum in its processes of financial colonisation in the aftermath of the Second World War, benefiting from the needs of a Europe brought to its knees by the conflict. It proved ultimately more advantageous to win new territory with Coca Cola, Kodak, or Ford and Chrysler motor cars than with military hardware.

The mutual suspicion and hostility between East and West was based on opposite political ideologies. These were expressed in the evident material contrasts between the affluence of the free West, where consumer culture suggested a freedom of political choice, albeit one soured by anti-communist paranoia, and the relative material deprivation of the ideologically subjugated East. Nowhere was this contrast more evident, nor mistrust more sharply defined, than in Berlin, a divided city in a divided country.

The Cold War was fought obliquely. It was fought as far as possible without direct confrontation. It was fought in the shadows, in the secret world of espionage, and, in the public arena, through the ritualised battle which was waged to conquer space. Both areas of conflict and competition were to enter the popular mythology of the Sixties and to play their part in shaping fantasy and reality. The imagery of the modern spy, the new technocrat locked in combat against the forces of evil, found form in the translation to film of Ian Fleming's hero, James Bond, an archetype of the Sixties.

James Bond, licensed to kill and to seduce, exploited a machismo image which pandered to a live-now-pay-later morality and to a fascination with sophisticated gadgetry. The latter, which came to the fore in the customised Aston Martin in *Goldfinger*, was to play an ever more important role in the Bond movies, to the detriment of Fleming's original stories, but presumably to the satisfaction of audiences highly attuned to the symbolism and status value of state-of-the-art appliances. Bond's adversaries tended to be maverick megalomaniacs, often sponsored by the East. They inhabited futuristic fantasy environments, such as the subterranean lair of Bond's first cinematic adversary, Dr No, or the chamber in which Goldfinger threatened to slice Bond in half with a laser beam. Set designer Ken Adam had the precise temperature of his market in creating these wish-fulfilment Sixties spaces.

The Space Race had a tremendous impact on the popular consciousness and on numerous facets of fashion,

Das internationale politische Geschehen der sechziger Jahre wurde vom kalten Krieg bestimmt. Der Lebensstandard im kommunistischen Ostblock stand im krassen Gegensatz zum realisierten amerikanischen Traum vom Überfluß, der auf der Wechselbeziehung von politischer und marktwirtschaftlicher Freiheit beruhte. In Amerika waren die Produzenten und die Konsumenten zum eigentlichen Motor des Staates geworden. Sie sorgten für die Energie und den Wohlstand, die den Erfolg dieser Nation begründeten. Darüber hinaus hatten die USA in der Nachkriegszeit durch die von ihnen betriebene fortschreitende »finanzielle Kolonisierung« beträchtlich an Boden gewonnen. Sie profitierten von den Bedürfnissen eines Europas, das der zweite Weltkrieg in die Knie gezwungen hatte. Letztlich erwies es sich als vorteilhafter, den Einflußbereich durch den Einsatz von Produkten wie Coca-Cola und Kodak oder Autos von Ford und Chrysler auszudehnen, als militärische Mittel einzusetzen.

Der gegenseitige Argwohn und die Feindseligkeit von Ost und West basierten auf den gegensätzlichen politischen Ideologien. Diese äußerten sich im offenkundigen materiellen Gegensatz zwischen dem Wohlstand des freien Westens, wo die Konsumkultur die – wenn auch durch den antikommunistischen Verfolgungswahn etwas getrübte – Freiheit der politischen Wahl suggerierte, und den materiellen Entbehrungen des ideologisch unterdrückten Ostens. Nirgendwo anders trat dieser Kontrast offener zutage und war das Mißtrauen stärker als in Berlin, der geteilten Stadt eines geteilten Landes.

Der kalte Krieg war ein indirekter Krieg, er fand soweit wie möglich ohne direkte Konfrontation statt. Ausgetragen wurde er im Untergrund, in der geheimen Welt der Spionage, und – ganz öffentlich – als ritualisierter Kampf um die Eroberung des Weltraums. Beide Kriegsschauplätze stimulierten in den sechziger Jahren die Mythologie des Alltags und wirkten entscheidend an der Ausgestaltung von Phantasie und Wirklichkeit mit. Die Vorstellung von einem modernen Agenten, einem neuen Technokraten, der in der Lage war, die Mächte des Bösen im Zaum zu halten, fand ihre Entsprechung in der Figur des James Bond. Dieser fiktive Held in den Romanen aus der Feder von Ian Fleming wurde zum Archetypus der sechziger Jahre.

Die Filmfigur James Bond mit der Lizenz zum Töten und Verführen hatte ein Macho-Image, das einer »Lebe jetzt, zahle später«-Moral huldigte. Gleichzeitig bediente sie sich der Faszination, die von hochentwickelten technischen Spielereien wie dem Sondermodell des Aston Martin in dem Film »Goldfinger« ausging. Die technischen Spezialeffekte spielten in den Bond-Filmen eine immer wichtigere Rolle. Obwohl sie in einem gewissen Widerspruch zu den Originalromanen von Ian Fleming standen, kamen sie bei den Kinobesuchern gut an, da diese für die Symbolik und den Statuswert von technisch ausgereiften Maschinen hochempfänglich waren. Die

En ce qui concerne la politique internationale, les années soixante se déroulèrent sur fond de guerre froide. Le rêve américain d'abondance prenait tout son relief face aux conditions de vie des pays communistes de l'Est. Dans la promesse américaine on entendait, implicitement, une corrélation entre liberté économique et liberté politique. L'industriel et le consommateur étaient devenus le moteur de l'Etat, la source d'énergie et de richesse qui conditionnait le succès national. Qui plus était, au sortir de la Seconde Guerre mondiale, les Etats-Unis, profitant des besoins d'une Europe que le conflit avait épuisée, étaient devenus une véritable force de domination financière. Il était finalement plus avantageux de conquérir des territoires grâce à Coca Cola, Kodak, Ford ou Chrysler qu'avec des armes lourdes. Méfiance et hostilité mutuelles entre Est et Ouest étaient fondées sur une opposition idéologique qui s'exprimait dans le contraste évident entre l'aisance matérielle de l'Ouest, où la culture de consommation semblait indiquer une liberté politique, assombrie parfois par la paranoïa anticommuniste, et la pauvreté matérielle relative de l'Est sous tutelle idéologique. Nulle part ce contraste n'était aussi marqué et cette méfiance aussi accentuée qu'à Berlin, ville déchirée dans un pays déchiré.

La guerre froide cherchait à éviter toute confrontation. Elle se menait dans l'ombre, dans l'univers secret de l'espionnage et, à découvert, dans l'affrontement ritualisé de la conquête de l'espace. La mythologie populaire des années soixante reflète ces deux tendances qui ont joué leur rôle dans l'élaboration du fantasme et de la réalité. L'imagerie de l'espion moderne, ce nouveau technocrate voué à une lutte contre les forces du mal, se retrouve tout entière dans le héros des films de Ian Fleming, James Bond, archétype des années soixante.

James Bond, payé pour tuer et pour séduire, justifiait son image machiste par une morale de vie au jour le jour et une fascination pour les gadgets sophistiqués. Ce dernier élément, qui apparaît avec l'Aston Martin suréquipée de «Goldfinger», allait jouer un rôle de plus en plus important dans la série de films James Bond, au détriment des histoires originales de Fleming, mais probablement pour le plus grand plaisir du public très sensible au symbolisme et au prestige de ces engins. Les adversaires de Bond sont des mégalomanes, souvent à la solde de l'Est. Ils habitent des lieux fantastiques, comme le repaire souterrain de Dr No ou le cabinet dans lequel Goldfinger menace le héros de le couper en deux au rayon laser. Le créateur des décors, Ken Adam, avait très exactement pris le pouls de son public en imaginant ces environnements fantaisistes.

La course à la conquête de l'espace eut un impact considérable sur la conscience populaire et détermina bien des facettes de la mode, du style et du design de la mi-décennie. L'idée que l'espace était à portée de main créait une ambiance d'optimisme et de respectueuse admiration. L'humanité semblait enfin capable d'utiliser

4

The Space Age – Science Fact and Science Fiction

Das Raumfahrtzeitalter – Science-Fact und Science-Fiction

L'ère de l'espace – Faits scientifiques et science-fiction

Sean Connery as James Bond,
1962

style and design in the mid-Sixties. The notion that the
conquest of space was within man's reach crystallised
the sense of optimism and awe of a world seemingly
able at last to harness highly refined technologies to
peaceful ambitions on so heroic a scale.

The U.S.S.R. had fired the opening salvo with the
launch in 1957 of Sputnik I, the first vehicle to travel
beyond the Earth's atmosphere. This was followed in
1961 by the U.S.S.R.'s success in launching the first
astronaut, Yuri Gagarin, into space. Kennedy took up the
challenge with his 1962 promise to land a man on the
moon before the end of the decade. The Space Race was
on, and NASA undertook a research and development
programme that became arguably the most sophisticated expression of the design process in human history.
The objective was clearly defined and was ultimately to
be achieved through the co-ordination of a myriad of
skills, not least the conceptual and organisational skills
which gave purpose and structure to the whole enter-
prise. Buoying the whole project was the unshakeable
faith in the possibility of realising the ambition which
Kennedy's words had inspired.

Space Age styles soon became the currency of fashionable design. Perhaps the most dramatic impact was in
the fashion world itself, in Paris couture. Paris fashion
had thrived on change, yet always within traditional para-
meters. In the mid-Sixties André Courrèges staged a
revolution with far-reaching effects. His spring 1965 collection changed the ground rules of fashion. His crisply
cut clothes, with plenty of white, sometimes striped in
black, short skirts, short white boots, slit-aperture white
sun glasses, were clothes for movement, for the young.
They were the antithesis of conventional status dressing.
Their context was the bright new world in which science
fiction was being transformed by technological progress
into science fact. These were the clothes of tomorrow
for which the world at last seemed ready. Courrèges,
brought up as an apprentice to Balenciaga in the grand
traditions of *haute couture*, was delivering Paris fashion
to a young, democratic future. His success was soon followed by that of Paco Rabanne, the Spanish-born Paris
couturier who came to prominence in 1966 with his
own interpretation of how to dress the liberated young
amazons of the Space Age. His proposal was a kind of
chain mail of plastic or light metal discs for clothes
which proved enormously newsworthy as expressive of
the futuristic mood. Meanwhile that great purist of Paris
fashion, Pierre Cardin, created his own version of the
Space Age look with stylised visored helmet hats and
clean-lined shift dresses.

Fashion photographers created a studio equivalent of
space with their strobe-lit seamless white backdrops.
These dazzling light-boxes without touch-points for the
figure articulated the concept of free movement in space.
Photographer Richard Avedon expressed the idea of the
white studio space as the new reality in the era of man's

Gegenspieler Bonds waren meist vom Osten protegierte,
größenwahnsinnige Einzelgänger. Sie bewohnten futuristische Phantasiebehausungen wie z. B. das unterirdische Versteck des ersten Bond-Gegners, Dr. No, oder
den Raum, in dem Goldfinger drohte, Bond mit einem
Laserstrahl zu zerteilen. Der Szenenbildner Ken Adam
hatte seinen Finger am Puls der Zeit. Die von ihm für die
Bond-Filme entworfenen Interieurs, die keinen Wunsch
offen ließen, entsprachen dem Traum der sechziger
Jahre.

Der Wettlauf um die Eroberung des Weltraums hatte
Mitte der sechziger Jahre enorme Auswirkungen auf das
allgemeine Bewußtsein der Menschen und damit auch
auf Mode, Stil und Design. Die Vorstellung, daß die
Eroberung des Weltraums im Bereich des Möglichen lag,
verstärkte den allgemeinen Optimismus und die Ehr-
furcht vor einer Welt, die allem Anschein nach endlich in
der Lage war, hochentwickelte Technologien in den
Dienst so weitgesteckter, friedlicher Ziele zu stellen.

Mit der Entsendung von Sputnik I, der 1957 als erster
Flugkörper die Erdatmosphäre verließ, hatten die UdSSR
den Startschuß zur Eroberung des Weltalls gegeben.
1961 konnte sie mit der erfolgreichen Aussendung von
Juri Gagarin, der als erster Astronaut in den Weltraum
geschossen wurde, einen weiteren Erfolg verbuchen.
Der amerikanische Präsident Kennedy nahm die Herausforderung an und versprach 1962, daß noch vor Ende
des Jahrzehnts ein Mensch auf dem Mond landen
werde. Der Wettlauf um die Eroberung des Weltalls war
damit im vollen Gange. Die NASA nahm mit ihrem
Forschungs- und Entwicklungsprogramm den wohl
umfangreichsten Planungsprozeß in der Geschichte der
Menschheit in Angriff. Das Planungsziel war klar umris-
sen und sollte schließlich durch den koordinierten Einsatz zahlloser Experten, nicht zuletzt durch den Einsatz
von Spezialisten für Konzeptentwicklung und Organisation, die dafür sorgten, daß das Unternehmen systematisch zum Ziel geführt werden konnte, erreicht werden.
Auftrieb gab dabei der unerschütterliche Glaube daran,
daß das von Kennedy formulierte ehrgeizige Vorhaben in
die Realität umgesetzt werden könnte.

Stilistische Anspielungen auf die Raumfahrt waren aus
dem Bereich der modernen Gestaltung schon bald nicht
mehr wegzudenken. Am deutlichsten traten sie in der
Welt der Mode zum Vorschein, wie etwa in der Pariser
Haute Couture. Die Pariser Mode hatte schon immer
von der Abwechslung gelebt, wenn auch im Rahmen
konventioneller Grenzen. Mitte der sechziger Jahre
sorgte André Courrèges jedoch für eine Revolution mit
weitreichenden Folgen. Seine Frühjahrskollektion 1965
veränderte die Grundlagen der Mode: Die flott geschnittenen Kreationen – überwiegend in Weiß oder auch
schwarz-weiß gestreift – mit kurzen Röcken, kurzen
weißen Stiefeln und weißen, nur mit einem Sehschlitz
versehenen Sonnenbrillen waren auf Bewegung ausgerichtet. Es war eine Mode für die Jugend, die sich bewußt

sa technologie de pointe à réaliser des ambitions pacifiques dans un registre véritablement héroïque.

L'U.R.S.S. avait tiré la première salve en lançant, en 1957, Spoutnik I, le premier vaisseau spatial à sortir de l'atmosphère terrestre. Puis en 1961, elle réussit à lancer dans l'espace le premier astronaute, Youri Gagarine. Kennedy releva le défi en promettant, en 1962, qu'un homme marcherait sur la lune avant la fin de la décennie. La course à l'espace avait commencé et la NASA entama un programme de recherche et de développement dont on peut dire qu'il est l'expression la plus sophistiquée du design de l'histoire de l'homme. L'objectif en était clair et serait atteint par la coordination d'une myriade de talents, dont conception et organisation, colonne vertébrale de toute l'entreprise, n'étaient pas les moindres. Le projet dans son ensemble reposait sur la ferme croyance que le rêve évoqué par Kennedy pouvait devenir réalité.

Le style de l'ère de l'espace devint très vite monnaie courante dans le design, plus intensément peut-être dans le monde de la mode, chez les couturiers parisiens. La mode, à Paris, avait toujours misé sur le changement mais toujours dans certaines limites. Au milieu de la décennie, André Courrèges fut l'instigateur d'une révolution qui allait être riche de conséquences. Sa collection du printemps 1965 bouleversa les règles du jeu. Ses vêtements à la coupe nette, très souvent blancs, parfois rayés de noir, jupes courtes, petites bottes blanches, lunettes de soleil blanches à lentilles en fente étaient faits pour le mouvement, pour la jeunesse. Ils allaient à l'encontre de tout ce qui était traditionnel. Leur contexte était ce monde tout beau, tout neuf dans lequel la science-fiction allait devenir réalité scientifique. C'étaient les vêtements de demain et on semblait enfin prêt à les porter. Courrèges, qui avait appris le métier chez Balenciaga dans le respect des traditions de la haute couture, dotait la mode parisienne d'un avenir jeune et démocratique. Son succès ouvrit la voie à Paco Rabanne, couturier parisien d'origine espagnole, qui fit sensation en 1966 par son interprétation de la mode pour les jeunes amazones de l'espace. Ses cottes de mailles de plastique ou de métal léger correspondaient au futurisme ambiant. A la même époque, ce grand puriste de la mode, Pierre Cardin, créait sa propre version du «look de l'espace» avec ses chapeaux-casques à visière et ses robes aux lignes simples et nettes.

Les photographes de mode firent à leur tour entrer l'aventure spatiale dans leur studio, avec des toiles de fond uniformément blanches, éclairées par des lampes stroboscopiques. Ces boîtes à lumière étincelantes où le corps n'avait plus aucun repère, évoquaient l'apesanteur. Pour le photographe Richard Avedon, l'espace blanc du studio représentait la réalité de l'ère du triomphe technologique. Ses photos sont le reflet exact des obsessions de l'époque: «Magnétisme lunaire», «La Fille des galaxies sur la lune», «Clarté lunaire», «The Young at

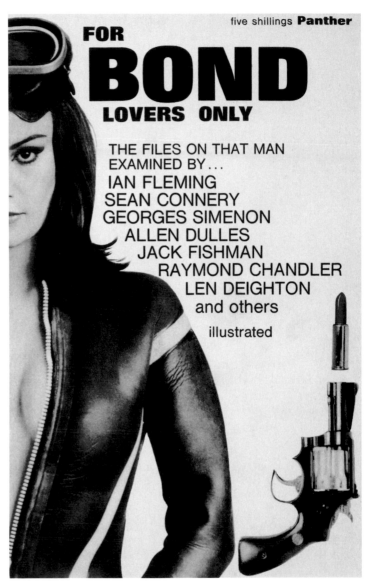

"For Bond Lovers Only", book cover, 1965

Metal halter dress, designed by **Paco Rabanne**, 1967

technological triumph. His photographs perfectly capture the obsessions of the Space Age in such images as "Moon Magnetics", "The Galactic Girl on the Moon", "Lunar Glow", "The Young at Zero Cool", and "The Galactic Beauty to the Rescue" in which Jean Shrimpton models a NASA space suit against a comic book space battle.

The Space Age was translated into visual fantasy on film in two contrasting productions, Roger Vadim's *Barbarella* (1967) and Stanley Kubrick's *2001 – A Space Odyssey* (1968). *Barbarella* is an erotic romp with the young Jane Fonda, dressed by Paco Rabanne, in the title role. Her space is a fantasy world of sensual, tactile surfaces, an organic dream bubble of plastics, fur and techno-sensual stimulation. It is exquisite hedonistic nonsense wrapped with great style in a fashionable iconography. *2001* is a more philosophically challenging riddle, but just as much of an indulgent visual feast. From the space station, a white space furnished with soft contoured seating designed by Olivier Mourgue, through the stylised space craft, and space uniforms which owe a debt to Courrèges, to the psychedelic landscape sequence, the film is a supreme evocation of an idea of space and space travel seen through late Sixties eyes.

White and silver were the colours of Space Age fashion. Distinguished examples of the look as adapted to furniture or object design must include Eero Aarnio's 1965 Globe chair; several manufacturers produced globe radios and televisions, in at least one instance with the workings visible within the perspex bubble. Viennese artist Walter Pichler created an archetypal Space Age design when he revised Le Corbusier's "Grand Confort" idea with the pierced aluminium frame of his 1966 "Galaxy I" armchair. Andy Warhol was ever attuned to fashion and in lining his Factory in silver and exhibiting helium-filled rectangular silver mylar balloons in 1966, he assimilated this Space Age reference into his Pop lexicon.

In 1969 American astronaut Neil Armstrong became the first man to set foot on the moon. The ambition had become a reality. But the dream was already tarnished. The Cold War had found Vietnam as an indirect point of aggression and the unbridled optimism which had characterised the early and mid-Sixties and the beginnings of the NASA space project had dissipated in the face of increased political disillusion.

The space programme gave a tremendous impetus to technological research and there were numerous by-products and lateral benefits through associated industries. Highly heat-resistant compounds, miniature circuitry and advanced computer technology were among the spin-offs. Computer graphics were developed within the aviation industry. William A. Fetter of the Boeing Airplane Company, Seattle, U.S.A., is credited with creating the first computer-generated "three dimensional" designs. Aviation design and research laid the foundations of today's computer-generated "virtual reality".

von der konventionellen, statusbetonenden Kleidung abgrenzen sollte. Sie war Bestandteil der schönen neuen Welt, in der mit Hilfe des technologischen Fortschritts Zukunftsphantasien in die Wirklichkeit übertragen wurden. Hier waren die Kleider der Zukunft entstanden, für die die Welt endlich bereit zu sein schien. Courrèges, der während seiner Ausbildung bei Balenciaga die großen Traditionen der Haute Couture kennengelernt hatte, führte die Pariser Mode in eine jugendliche, demokratische Zukunft. Auf den Erfolg von Courrèges folgte schon bald der Triumph des spanischen Modeschöpfers Paco Rabanne, der 1966 mit seiner persönlichen Interpretation einer Mode für die jungen, emanzipierten Amazonen des Raumfahrtzeitalters berühmt wurde. Seine hochaktuellen Schöpfungen waren in Form von Kettenhemden aus Plastik- oder Leichtmetallscheiben gearbeitet. Sie brachten die futuristische Stimmung perfekt zum Ausdruck. Gleichzeitig schuf Pierre Cardin, der große Purist unter den Pariser Couturiers, eine eigenständige Variante des Raumfahrer-Looks. Typisches Merkmal seiner Entwürfe waren die Hüte in Form von stilisierten, visierbewehrten Helmen oder die helmartigen Schirmmützen in Verbindung mit schlicht geschnittenen Hängekleidern.

Die Modefotografen schufen in ihren Studios eine eigene Weltraumatmosphäre. Mit elektronischen Blitzgeräten hell angestrahlte Wände bildeten einen nahtlosen, weißen Hintergrund. In diesen blendenden Lichtkammern gab es keine Berührungspunkte mehr mit der zu fotografierenden Person. Sie vermittelten den Eindruck der Schwerelosigkeit im All. Der Fotograf Richard Avedon verstand den weißen Studioraum als Ausdruck einer neuen Realität in einer Zeit, die vom Triumph der Technologie bestimmt wurde. Avedon wirkte 1965 als Gast-Herausgeber an der Gestaltung des Aprilheftes von »Harper's Bazaar« mit. Seine dort publizierten Fotografien, etwa »Moon Magnetics« oder »The Young at Zero Cool« und »The Galactic Beauty to the Rescue«, auf der Jean Shrimpton in einem NASA-Raumanzug vor dem Hintergrund einer Comic-Weltraumschlacht posiert, halten den Geist des Raumfahrtzeitalters auf perfekte Weise fest.

Das Raumfahrtzeitalter wurde in zwei recht gegensätzlichen Filmen, »Barbarella« von Roger Vadim (1967) und »2001 – Odyssee im Weltraum« von Stanley Kubrick (1968), zum Gegenstand der visuellen Phantasie. In der erotischen Filmkomödie »Barbarella« spielt die junge Jane Fonda in Kostümen von Paco Rabanne die Titelrolle. Sie bewegt sich in einer Phantasiewelt voll von sinnlichen, tastbaren Oberflächen – einer organischen Traumblase aus Kunststoffen, Pelzen und technischansprechenden Reizen. Das Ergebnis ist ein ausgezeichneter filmischer Unsinn über die Sinnenlust, der stilistisch gekonnt in eine moderne Ikonographie verpackt ist. Der rätselhafte Film »2001« veranlaßt eher zu philosophischen Betrachtungen, stellt aber nichtsdestoweni-

Zero Cool», et «Beauté galactique à la rescousse», cliché pour lequel Jean Shrimpton porte une combinaison d'astronaute de la NASA sur un fond de guerre des étoiles en bande dessinée.

L'ère spatiale fut illustrée par deux films très différents, «Barbarella» (1967) de Roger Vadim et «2001 – Odyssée de l'espace» (1968) de Stanley Kubrick. Le premier est une fable érotique dont l'héroïne est la jeune Jane Fonda, habillée par Paco Rabanne. L'espace y est un univers de fantaisie, bulle onirique faite de plastique, de fourrure et d'érotisme techno-sensuel. C'est une histoire légère et absurde, très habilement présentée dans un emballage iconographique à la mode. «2001» pose un problème plus philosophique, mais le film a, lui aussi, été fait pour le plaisir de l'œil. De la station spatiale, un espace blanc meublé par les sièges aux contours arrondis de Olivier Mourgue, au vaisseau stylisé et aux uniformes, très inspirés de Courrèges, jusqu'à la séquence tournée dans un paysage psychédélique, le film représente très exactement l'idée de l'espace et du voyage spatial qui était celle de la fin des années soixante.

Le blanc et l'argent étaient les couleurs à la mode. Dans le domaine du design de meubles et d'objets, il faut citer la Chaise-globe (1965) d'Eero Aarnio. On vit apparaître des radios-globes et des télévisions-globes, et, dans l'un des cas au moins, tous les branchements étaient visibles dans la bulle de plexi. L'artiste viennois Walter Pichler, s'inspirant du fauteuil «Grand confort» de Le Corbusier, créa en 1966 avec son siège «Galaxy I» au cadre en aluminium perforé, un archétype du design spatial. Comme toujours en phase avec la mode, Andy Warhol recouvrit les murs de sa Factory d'un revêtement argenté et, exposant en 1966 des ballons à l'hélium rectangulaires et de couleur argent, intégra ainsi sa référence à l'ère spatiale dans son lexique pop.

En 1969, l'astronaute américain Neil Armstrong devint le premier homme à marcher sur la Lune. Le rêve était devenu réalité. Mais les choses ne tardèrent pas à se gâter. Avec le Vietnam la guerre froide avait trouvé une façon détournée de passer à l'offensive et l'optimisme débridé, qui avait caractérisé cette première moitié de la décennie et le début du programme spatial de la NASA, s'était évanoui. Politiquement, on était en pleine désillusion. Le programme spatial donna une impulsion très forte à la recherche technologique; de nombreux produits dérivés apparurent et les industries associées à la recherche jouirent de bénéfices secondaires. Parmi ces produits-ricochets: des composés résistants à une chaleur intense, des circuits miniaturisés, des techniques informatiques de pointe. Le dessin par ordinateur se développa dans le cadre de l'industrie aéronautique. On attribue à William A. Fetter, de la Boeing Airplane Company à Seattle, USA, la création des premiers schémas tridimensionnels sur ordinateur. Le design et la recherche aéronautiques établirent les fondations de ce qui allait devenir notre «réalité virtuelle».

Space-age fashion from **André Courrèges'** spring 1965 collection, published by The Observer, 7 March 1965

1963 Russian Vostok programme cosmonauts,
Yuri Gagarin second from left

ger eine grandiose Augenweide dar. In allen Bereichen des Films, in der Weltraumstation – eine weiße Halle, die mit sanft abgerundeten Sitzmöbeln nach Entwürfen von Olivier Mourgue eingerichtet ist –, in dem stilisierten Raumfahrzeug, in den von Courrèges-Modellen inspirierten Raumfahrtanzügen und in den Sequenzen von psychedelischen Landschaftsbildern leben die Vorstellungen vom Weltraum und von der Raumfahrt aus der Sicht der späten sechziger Jahre auf.

Die Farben Weiß und Silber dominierten das Design des Raumfahrtzeitalters. Zu den herausragenden Möbeln und Objekten, die in diesem Stil entstanden, zählen Eero Aarnios »Globe-Sessel« aus dem Jahr 1965 und die kugelförmigen Radio- und Fernsehapparate, die von verschiedenen Herstellern produziert wurden. Bei mindestens einem Fabrikat gab das runde Plexiglasgehäuse den Blick auf das technische Innenleben frei. Dem Wiener Künstler Walter Pichler gelang mit seinem Sessel »Galaxy I« ein mustergültiger Archetypus im Raumfahrt-Look, indem er Le Corbusiers Sesselentwurf »Grand Confort« adaptierte und mit einem neuen Rahmengerüst aus perforiertem Aluminium versah. Andy Warhol, der sich stets vom modischen Zeitgeschmack inspirieren ließ, verkleidete die Innenräume seiner »Factory« mit silberfarbenen Materialien und ließ hier 1966 rechteckige, mit Helium gefüllte Ballons aus silberner Plastikfolie aufsteigen. Mit diesen Aktionen nahm er das Vokabular des Raumfahrtzeitalters in sein Pop-Repertoire auf.

Im Jahr 1969 betrat der amerikanische Astronaut Neil Armstrong als erster Mensch den Mond. Der ehrgeizige Traum war in Erfüllung gegangen und hatte dennoch bereits an Glanz verloren. In Vietnam war der kalte Krieg in einen offenen Krieg umgeschlagen, was dazu führte, daß sich der überschwengliche Optimismus, der die frühen und mittleren sechziger Jahre sowie die Anfänge des NASA-Projektes geprägt hatte, angesichts der wachsenden politischen Enttäuschung verflüchtigte.

Das Raumfahrtprogramm wirkte wie ein gewaltiger Schrittmacher auf die technologische Forschung. Die am Programm beteiligten Industrien stießen im Verlaufe ihrer Forschungen auf zahlreiche Nebenprodukte, die später von hohem Nutzen waren. Zu diesen Produkten zählten stark hitzebeständige Legierungen, elektronische Miniaturschaltkreise und die hochentwickelte Computertechnologie. Die Flugzeugindustrie entwickelte die Computergrafik. William A. Fetter von der Flugzeugfirma Boeing im amerikanischen Seattle kommt der Verdienst zu, sich als erster mit computergestützten »dreidimensionalen« Konstruktionszeichnungen beschäftigt zu haben. Die Planungen und die Forschungen der Flugzeugindustrie haben die Grundlagen für die computererzeugte »virtual reality« von heute geschaffen.

Scene from the film "2001:
A Space Odyssey" by Stanley
Kubrick, 1968

Yuri Gagarin, the world's first astronaut, 1968

Space-age heroines decorate panels during construction of a new shop by Hans Hollein, Vienna, 1966

LEFT
"Eclipse" lamp, designed by **Vico Magistretti** for Artemide, 1967

PAGE **103**
Astronaut Edwin A. Aldrin Jr., Apollo 11 mission, 1969

Space-age helmet hat,
designed by **Pierre Cardin**,
c. 1966

Metal trouser suit, designed
by **Paco Rabanne**, 1969

PAGE **105**
Metal dress, designed by **Paco
Rabanne**, 1969

Mary Quant's white interior,
c. 1966

Jill Kennington in a space-age
science fiction advertisement
for lipstick, 1967

PAGE 107
The fashion for silver,
illustrated in "Nova",
September 1966

Rocker, designed by
Marc Held, 1970

"Téléavia" television, designed
by **Roger Tallon**, 1963

TOP
Asko "Pastilli" chair, designed
by **Eero Aarnio**, fibreglass,
1968

BOTTOM
Asko bubble chair, designed
by **Eero Aarnio**, 1965

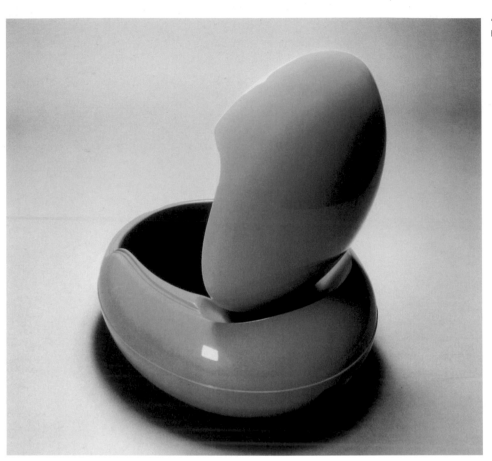

"Egg" garden chair, designed by **Peter Ghyczy**, 1968

"Tappo Kontakt" record player, anonymous

PAGE 111
Lamp, designed by **Gae Aulenti**, metal, 1969

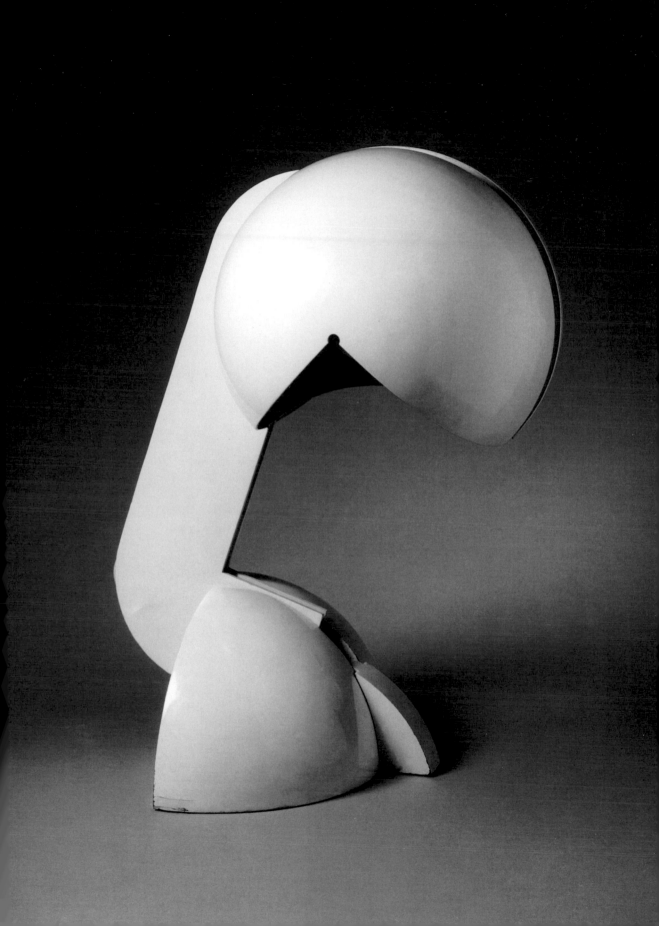

TOP
"Kantarelli" table, designed by
Eero Aarnio, 1965

BOTTOM
Globe television, retailed by
Zarach, London, late 1960s

PAGE **113**
"Globe" chair, designed by
Eero Aarnio, 1965

Scene from the film "Goldfinger", designed by **Ken
Adam,** 1964

"Moon" lamp and wire chairs,
designed by **Verner Panton,**
1960

PAGE **115**
Central living block of the
"Wohnmodell 1969", designed
by **Joe Colombo,** shown at the
"Visiona" exhibition by Bayer
AG, 1969

"Lunar rocket" fabric,
designed by **Eddie Squire**
for Warner's, c. 1969–70

Chair, designed by **Roger
Tallon**, 1965, produced by
Jacques Lacloche, Paris

Poster for "Barbarella", 1967

Jane Fonda as Barbarella, 1967

THIS PAGE AND PAGE **119** TOP
Scenes from the film "2001:
A Space Odyssey" by Stanley
Kubrick, 1968

PAGE **119** BOTTOM
"Djinn" chair and stool,
designed by **Olivier Mourgue**,
1965

"Grillo" telephone, designed
by **Marco Zanuso** and **Richard
Sapper**, 1965

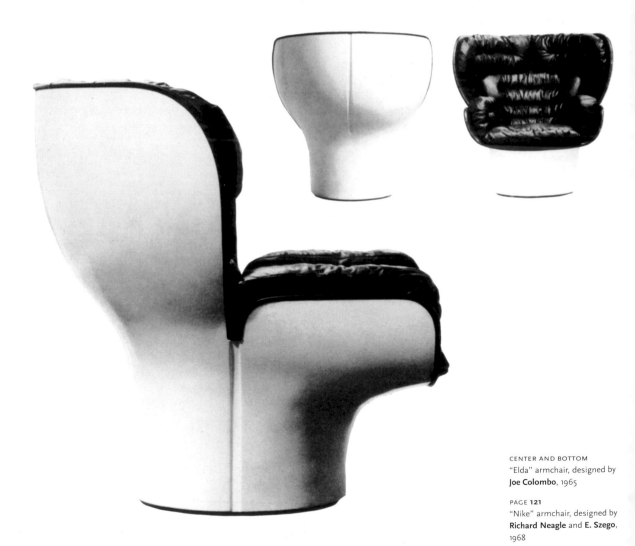

"Elda" armchair, designed by
Joe Colombo, 1965

PAGE **121**
"Nike" armchair, designed by
Richard Neagle and **E. Szego**,
1968

"Alda" armchair, designed
by **Cesare Casati** and **Enzo
Hybsch**, 1966

"Galaxy 1" armchair, designed
by **Walter Pichler**, aluminium
and leather, 1966

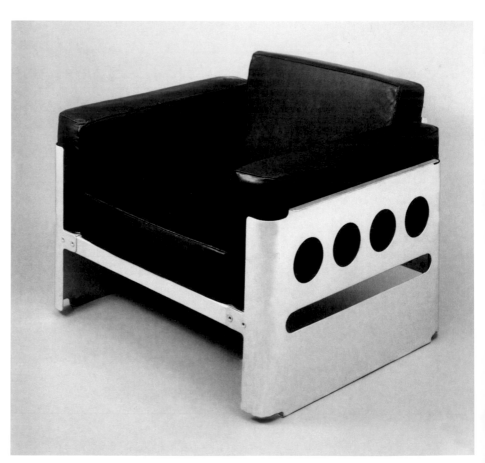

"Rotoliving" night environment for Sormani with
"Cabriolet" bed, designed by
Joe Colombo, 1969, produced
from 1971

TOP
"Simone" sofa, designed by
Cesare Casati, 1966, poduced
by Comfort

BOTTOM
Office desk, designed by
Maurice Calka, 1969

PAGE **125**
Computer-generated graphics
charting body movements for
Boeing

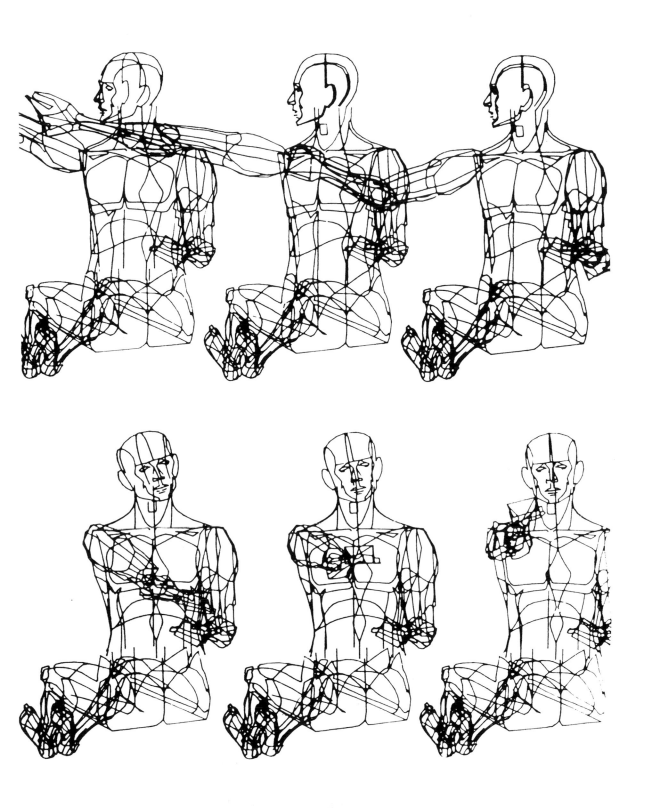

As prosperity increased after the initial austerity of the post-war years, the immediate need to rebuild and the urgency of keeping up with housing demand became overlaid with more complex and systematic urban planning. Stop-gap replacement programmes were overtaken by ambitious schemes to explore and redefine the functions and forms of cities. The International Style had proposed an architecture of prestige corporate or institutional headquarters, but there was far more to city planning than the steel and glass towers which marked the new business or civic centres. Central to the preoccupations of many architects and planners through the Sixties were utopian ideals of transforming traditional cities into grandiose visions corresponding to a proposed new way of living.

The guiding principles of such cities had been established and nurtured in the Twenties and Thirties by Le Corbusier. Given the opportunity, Le Corbusier would readily have levelled the haphazard intricacies of our old cities, built up through centuries and largely conceived around pedestrian or horse transport. In their place, he and his disciples saw order reigning supreme in a geometric pattern of living, working, administrative and trading towers set in parklands intersected by motor transit corridors. The vision had become a reality at the beginning of the decade with the completion of the Brasilia project, a capital city conceived in its entirety on the drawing board by a team led by Lucia Costa and Oscar Niemeyer. Brasilia, with its dramatic forms and vistas, was a powerful statement of faith. It was a monument to an idea. It was also a hostile, impersonal environment in which to live or work. Individual expression or choice were subsumed to the imposed collective good.

The Corbusian credo enjoyed considerable support and provided the justification for the wholesale destruction and reconstruction through the Sixties of many town and city centres and dense residential areas. In their place came impersonal shopping precincts and tower block housing. Urban dreams of light, space and a new social order were discredited by the realities of bleak towers and characterless, draughty open spaces. Crystal spires of the imagination translated into the brutality of weather-beaten reinforced concrete. The high moral tone of Le Corbusier's theorizing was systematically compromised by unscrupulous developers and incompetent or corrupt planning authorities. By the close of the decade a deep reaction had set in.

The fundamental flaws of what had become an arrogant and exploitative paternalism were now increasingly evident. The problems of adapting old city centres to changing usages, particularly also to the dramatic increase of motor traffic, were well recognised. Intelligent programmes or rationalised, highly legible road and motorway sign systems were one beneficial by-product of applying national design master plans. But urban

In dem Maße, in dem nach den entbehrungsreichen Nachkriegsjahren der Wohlstand zurückkehrte, löste eine umfassendere und systematischere Städteplanung die reinen Wiederaufbaumaßnahmen ab, die aufgrund der Wohnungsnot erforderlich waren. Die Sofortprogramme zur Wiederbeschaffung von Wohnraum wurden durch ehrgeizige Projekte abgelöst, in denen man die Funktion und die Gestaltung von Städten zu erforschen und neu zu definieren suchte. Der Internationale Stil hatte eine Prestigearchitektur hervorgebracht, die ihren Ausdruck in den Verwaltungsgebäuden von Konzernen und Institutionen fand. Städteplanung bedeutete jedoch wesentlich mehr als das reine Entwerfen der Stahl- und Glastürme, von denen die neuen Geschäfts- und Verwaltungszentren geprägt wurden. Während der sechziger Jahre richtete sich das Interesse vieler Architekten und Planer hauptsächlich darauf, ihre utopischen Ideale zu verwirklichen. Entsprechend ihren Visionen wollten sie jahrhundertealte, gewachsene Städte in grandiose Gebilde verwandeln, die dem neuen Lebensstil gerecht wurden.

Die theoretischen Grundlagen für solche Städte waren von Le Corbusier bereits in den zwanziger und dreißiger Jahren erarbeitet und weiterentwickelt worden. Wäre es Le Corbusier möglich gewesen, hätte er schon damals die über Jahrhunderte gewachsenen, verwinkelten Gassen und Straßen unserer alten Städte, die fast alle nur für Fußgänger und Pferde ausgelegt waren, dem Erdboden gleichgemacht. An ihrer Stelle hätten er und seine Schüler in parkähnlichen, mit Verkehrsschneisen durchzogenen, geometrisch angelegten Anlagen riesige Wohn-, Arbeits-, Verwaltungs- und Einkaufszentren errichtet. Anfang der sechziger Jahre wurde ihre Vision mit der Fertigstellung des Brasilia-Projekts Realität. Die brasilianische Hauptstadt ist in ihrer Gesamtheit von einem Architektenteam unter der Leitung von Lucia Costa und Oscar Niemeyer entworfen worden. Brasilia mit seinen spektakulären Silhouetten und eindrucksvollen Perspektiven ist ein gewaltiges Glaubensbekenntnis, das Denkmal einer Idee. Diejenigen aber, die dort wohnen oder arbeiten müssen, empfinden die Stadt als abweisend und unpersönlich. Die Selbstverwirklichung und die freie Wahl des Individuums sind dem Diktat des kollektiven Wohls unterworfen worden.

Die städtebaulichen Visionen Le Corbusiers erfreuten sich in den sechziger Jahren großer Beliebtheit und lieferten die Rechtfertigung für den Abriß und den anschließenden Wiederaufbau ganzer Orts- und Stadtzentren. Dichtbesiedelte Wohngebiete mußten unpersönlichen Einkaufszentren und Wohnhochhäusern weichen. Die städtebaulichen Träume von Helligkeit, Raum und einer neuen Gesellschaftsordnung gerieten jedoch angesichts der Realität von düsteren Wohnblocks und charakterlosen, zugigen Plätzen schon bald in Verruf. Die als gläserne Türme geplanten Wohnblocks wurden von der Brutalität des verwitternden Stahlbetons

Après l'austérité des premières années de l'après-guerre, prospérité aidant, la reconstruction, qui avait dû d'abord faire face aux besoins immédiats en logements, se fit plus systématique. A la place de simples programmes «bouche-trous» on vit naître d'ambitieux projets qui remettaient en question fonctions et configurations urbaines. Le Style International donna naissance à de prestigieux quartiers généraux industriels et administratifs mais l'urbanisme ne consistait pas seulement en ces tours d'acier et de verre des nouveaux centres urbains. Au cours des années soixante, bien des architectes et des urbanistes s'étaient penchés sur les idéaux utopiques transformant l'habitat urbain traditionnel en visions grandioses à la mesure d'une nouvelle manière de vivre.

Les principes fondateurs de ce type de projets visionnaires avaient été énoncés et élaborés pendant les années vingt et trente par Le Corbusier. S'il en avait eu la possibilité, l'architecte aurait été prêt à raser les quartiers tortueux de nos vieilles villes, construites au long des siècles pour une circulation de piétons ou de véhicules tirés par des chevaux. En leur place, ses disciples et lui imaginaient un ordre qui régnerait sans partage selon un schéma géométrique fait de tours à vivre, à travailler, de blocs administratifs et commerciaux disposés sur des espaces verts, traversés par des couloirs de transit automobile. Cette vision était devenue réalité à l'aube de la décennie lorsque fut construite Brasília, capitale conçue entièrement sur la planche à dessin par une équipe dirigée par Lucia Costa et Oscar Niemeyer. Avec ses lignes hardies et ses belles perspectives cette ville était une profession de foi, un monument élevé à une idée. Mais c'était aussi un environnement sans chaleur, impersonnel. L'expression ou le choix individuel y étaient sacrifiés à une notion artificielle du bien commun.

Le credo de Le Corbusier fut repris par bien des architectes et servit d'alibi pendant les années soixante à la destruction sans merci et à la reconstruction de plus d'une ville, plus d'un centre urbain et plus d'un quartier résidentiel. A leur place s'élevèrent des centres commerciaux impersonnels et des tours d'appartements. Le rêve d'une ville claire et aérée, d'un nouvel ordre social fut chassé par la réalité: bâtiments tristes, sans caractère, espaces balayés par le vent. Les flèches de cristal de l'imagination transformées en béton armé brutal et suintant. Le discours d'une haute portée morale de Le Corbusier fut systématiquement discrédité par des investisseurs sans scrupules et des autorités d'urbanisme incompétentes ou corrompues. Vers la fin de la décennie, une réaction virulente s'était déclarée.

Les faiblesses de ce qui était devenu un paternalisme sans vergogne étaient de plus en plus évidentes. Les problèmes rencontrés en cherchant à adapter le centre des villes anciennes aux mœurs de l'époque, et surtout à une augmentation formidable de la circulation automo-

5

Urban Dreams –
Urban Realities

Urbane Träume –
Urbane Wirklichkeit

La ville rêvée –
La ville vécue

design issues were increasingly perceived as requiring pragmatic, fluid solutions, determined by plebiscite rather than diktat.

Theo Crosby, architect, designer and theorist, had written in 1965 in *Architecture: city sense*, that "the only way visually and socially dynamic cities can be brought about is by the correct marshalling of constructive forces… a hierarchy of planner, architect, artist". A decade later, in a lecture *The Pessimist Utopia*, his point of view had mellowed as he expressed his obsession with "the idea of the ordinary, the miracle of normality, the intricate, complex mechanisms of our bodies and the equally miraculous mechanisms of cities, or markets, of that whole process of interaction, which makes up our ordinary lives". In 1972 architects Robert Venturi, Denise Scott Brown and Steven Izenour published their commentary on the recent ills of much architectural practice. They wrote, in the introduction to *Learning from Las Vegas*, "Architects are out of the habit of looking non-judgementally at the environment, because orthodox modern architecture is progressive, if not revolutionary, utopian and puristic; it is dissatisfied with existing conditions. Modern architecture has been anything but permissive: architects have preferred to change the existing environment rather than enhance what is there". Venturi and his colleagues recognised the need to integrate old and new, to respect the layering of cities, the sign systems and advertising, the vernacular as well as the purist architecture.

The dogmatism of autocratic Modernist visionaries was challenged by architects who respected the organic, evolutionary aspects of the city. These included the Japanese "Metabolists" whose label acknowledges the almost biological aspect of their principle of cities needing to develop as living organisms. Kisho Kurokawa's 1961 "Helix" city was precisely such a project which could grow organically as need required. Perhaps the most inventive and influential thinkers in this vein were the members of the British Archigram group, comprising Warren Chalk, Peter Cook, Dennis Crompton, David Greene, Ron Herron and Michael Webb. Their ideas were expressed in imaginative design projects in the pages of their eponymous journal, first published in 1961. They borrowed from science fiction, from engineering, from outside their own medium in order to re-invigorate the idea of architecture. In *Amazing Archigram 4 Zoom Issue* (1964), Warren Chalk wrote: "In this second half of the twentieth century, the old idols are crumbling, the old precepts strangely irrelevant, the old dogmas no longer valid. We are in pursuit of an idea, a new vernacular, something to stand alongside the space capsules, computers, and throw-away packages of an atomic and electronic age".

Expo '67, staged in Montreal, provided a context in which architects could explore these new possibilities, exploiting advanced engineering technologies in

eingeholt. Skrupellose Baulöwen und inkompetente oder korrupte Planungsbehörden untergruben systematisch den hohen moralischen Anspruch der von Le Corbusier erarbeiteten architektonischen Konzeption. Gegen Ende der sechziger Jahre setzte eine tiefgreifende Reaktion ein.

Die grundsätzlichen Mängel dessen, was sich zu einer arroganten und ausbeuterischen Bevormundung entwickelt hatte, traten nun immer deutlicher zutage. Man erkannte die Probleme der Anpassung alter Stadtkerne an die neuen Anforderungen, insbesondere an den drastisch wachsenden Autoverkehr. Zwar erwiesen sich die intelligenten Programme für logische, gut lesbare Straßenbeschilderungssysteme als nützliche Begleiterscheinungen der überregionalen Planung, die Probleme der Städteplanung verlangten jedoch nach pragmatischen und flexiblen Lösungen, und diese ließen sich eher »von unten«, auf demokratischem Wege, als durch ein Diktat »von oben« erreichen.

Der Architekt, Designer und Theoretiker Theo Crosby schrieb 1965 in »Architecture: city sense«: »Die einzige Möglichkeit, optisch und gesellschaftlich dynamische Städte zu verwirklichen, ist der sinnvolle Einsatz konstruktiver Kräfte … einer Hierarchie von Planern, Architekten und Künstlern.« Ein Jahrzehnt später vertrat er in seinem Vortrag »The Pessimist Utopia« (»Die Utopie des Pessimisten«) einen abgeklärteren Standpunkt. Er erläuterte seine Besessenheit von »der Idee des Alltäglichen, dem Wunder der Normalität, dem kunstvollen, komplexen Mechanismus unseres Körpers und den ebenso erstaunlichen Mechanismen der Städte und Märkte, von diesem ganzen Interaktionsprozeß, der unser alltägliches Leben ausmacht«. 1972 veröffentlichten die Architekten Robert Venturi, Denise Scott Brown und Steven Izenour ihren Kommentar zu den gegenwärtigen Mißständen in der Architektur. In der Einführung zu »Learning from Las Vegas« (»Lernen von Las Vegas«) schrieben sie: »Die Architekten haben die Fähigkeit verloren, ihre Umgebung vorurteilslos wahrzunehmen, denn die orthodoxe Architektur der Moderne hatte fortschrittlich, wenn nicht sogar revolutionär, utopisch oder puristisch zu sein. Diese Architektur war unzufrieden mit den bestehenden Verhältnissen und alles andere als tolerant. Die Architekten zogen es vor, die vorhandene Architektur umzugestalten, anstatt das, was sie vorfanden, vorteilhaft zur Geltung zu bringen.« Venturi und seine Kollegen erkannten die Notwendigkeit, das Alte mit dem Neuen zu verbinden. Sie akzeptierten die gewachsenen Strukturen der Städte mit ihren Zeichensystemen und Reklametafeln, mit ihren sowohl traditionellen als auch puristischen Architekturen.

Der Dogmatismus der selbstherrlichen modernistischen Visionäre stellte für jene Architekten eine Herausforderung dar, die das organische, historisch gewachsene Erscheinungsbild einer Stadt zu würdigen wußten. Zu ihnen zählten die japanischen »Metabolisten«, die in bezug auf die Stadtplanung das beinahe biologische

bile, étaient bien connus. L'application de programmes de design nationaux déboucha, entre autres, sur une signalétique rationnelle et bien lisible sur routes et autoroutes. Mais il était de plus en plus clair que les problèmes seraient résolus de façon pragmatique et souple, par consensus, plutôt que de façon autoritaire.

Theo Crosby, architecte, designer et théoricien, avait écrit en 1965 dans «Architecture: city sense» que «la seule façon dont on pourra faire naître des villes esthétiquement et socialement dynamiques, ce sera par la coopération réussie des forces de la construction ... une hiérarchie faite d'urbanistes, d'architectes et d'artistes.» Dix ans plus tard, dans une conférence intitulée «The Pessimist Utopia», il avait étoffé son point de vue et il se montra très préoccupé par «l'idée de l'ordinaire, le miracle de la normalité, les mécanismes subtils, complexes de notre corps et ceux, également miraculeux, des cités, des marchés, de tout ce processus d'interaction qui tisse notre vie quotidienne». En 1972, les architectes Robert Venturi, Denise Scott Brown et Steven Izenour publièrent un commentaire sur certaines récentes erreurs architecturales. Dans l'introduction de leur texte «Learning from Las Vegas» ils écrivirent: «Si les architectes ont perdu l'habitude de regarder leur environnement sans le critiquer, c'est parce que l'architecture moderne est par nature progressiste, sinon révolutionnaire, utopiste et puriste; elle ne peut se satisfaire des conditions existantes. L'architecture moderne a été tout sauf permissive: on a préféré le changement radical à l'amélioration de ce qui existait déjà». Venturi et ses confrères reconnaissaient l'utilité de faire coexister ancien et moderne, de respecter le processus de formation des villes, les systèmes signalétiques publicitaires, l'architecture indigène autant que l'architecture puriste.

Le dogmatisme des visionnaires-autocrates du modernisme fut mis en question par des architectes qui respectaient les aspects organiques, évolutifs de la ville. Parmi eux, les «métabolistes» japonais qui, comme leur nom l'indique, voient dans la ville quelque chose de biologique qui doit se développer comme un organisme vivant. La cité «Helix» (1961) de Kisho Kurokawa était précisément cela: un projet qui pouvait connaître une croissance organique, en rapport avec les besoins. Dans cette veine, les penseurs, qui furent peut-être les plus inventifs et les plus influents, furent les membres du groupe britannique Archigram, Warren Chalk, Peter Cook, Dennis Crompton, David Greene, Ron Herron et Michael Webb. En 1961, ils publièrent dans le journal du même nom des projets pleins d'imagination. Ils s'inspiraient de la science-fiction, du design industriel, de disciplines extérieures à la leur pour revigorer l'idée de l'architecture. Dans «Amazing Archigram 4 Zoom Issue» (1964) Warren Chalk écrivit: «Dans cette seconde moitié du vingtième siècle, les vieilles idoles s'écroulent, les vieux préceptes n'ont plus rien à nous dire, les vieux dogmes n'ont plus cours. Nous courons après une idée,

Congress Building and Administration Block on the Plaza dos tres Poderes in Brasilia, designed by **Oscar Niemeyer**, 1958

The Supreme Federal Court building, Brasilia, designed by **Oscar Niemeyer**, 1958–60

dramatic, symbolic structures. Buckminster Fuller's geodesic dome, Moshe Safdie's modular "Habitat" scheme and the tent-like German pavilion by Rolf Gutbrod and Frei Otto with its steel poles and netting and plastic membrane, marked a search for an expressive and appropriate architectural language.

Venturi had addressed the vital issues of symbol and metaphor in his 1966 study *Complexity and Contradiction in Architecture*. At the same time there emerged another strong challenge to the Modernist canon, that of the two architectural design practices, Archizoom and Superstudio, both founded in 1966 in a context of intense student political debate within the Faculty of Architecture at Florence. These studios recognised the complexities and contradictions in architecture, and saw it as a discipline which could not function in isolation. They became think-tanks for progressive Italian design theory, looking upon city planning as the basis of wide-ranging philosophical discussions, in the words of Archizoom founder member and spokesman Andrea Branzi, investigating "the new Pop scene" whilst not excluding "architecture as a political instrument". The architect had acquired a role and a responsibility as shaman in a society with complex spiritual and emotional as well as material and practical needs.

Prinzip vertraten, nach dem sich Städte wie lebende Organismen entwickeln durften. Das 1961 von Kisho Kurokawa entwickelte »Helix«-City-Projekt war der Entwurf einer Stadt, die bei Bedarf organisch wachsen konnte. Die vielleicht innovativsten und einflußreichsten Denker auf diesem Gebiet waren die Mitglieder der englischen Architektengruppe Archigram, zu denen Warren Chalk, Peter Cook, Dennis Crompton, David Greene, Ron Herron und Michael Webb gehörten. Ihre Vorstellungen äußerten sich in der Verbreitung von imaginären Design-Projekten, die sie in ihrer gleichnamigen Zeitschrift (»Archigram«), die 1961 zum ersten Mal erschien, veröffentlichten. Im »Amazing Archigram 4 Zoom Issue« (1964) faßte Warren Chalk das so zusammen: »Heute, in der zweiten Hälfte des 20. Jahrhunderts, stürzen die alten Idole in sich zusammen, sind die alten Gebote seltsam belanglos geworden, die alten Dogmen nicht mehr gültig. Wir sind auf der Jagd nach einer neuen Idee, einem eigenen Ausdruck, nach etwas, was neben den Raumkapseln, Computern und Wegwerfartikeln unseres elektronischen Atomzeitalters bestehen kann.«

Die Weltausstellung 1967 in Montreal eröffnete den beteiligten Architekten die Gelegenheit, modernste Konstruktionstechnologien für ihre spektakulären Bauten zu nutzen. Buckminster Fullers geodätische Kuppel, Moshe Safdies »Habitat«-Terassenblock sowie der von Rolf Gutbrod und Frei Otto in Form einer Zeltkonstruktion errichtete deutsche Pavillon mit seinen Stahlpfosten, seiner Verspannung und seiner Plastikhaut waren typisch für die Suche nach einer ausdrucksstarken und angemessenen architektonischen Formensprache.

Venturi setzte sich bereits 1966 in seiner Studie »Complexity and Contradiction in Architecture« (»Komplexität und Widerspruch in der Architektur«) mit der Kernfrage nach Symbol und Metapher auseinander. Gleichzeitig stellten auch die Architektur- und Designbüros Archizoom und Superstudio, die aus den politischen Studentenprotesten in der Architekturfakultät der Universiät Florenz 1966 hervorgegangen waren, die modernistischen Prinzipien in Frage. Beide Büros waren sich der Komplexität und der Widersprüchlichkeit der Architektur bewußt und verstanden diese als eine Fachrichtung, die allein auf sich gestellt, nicht bestehen könnte. Archizoom und Superstudio entwickelten sich zu Denkfabriken der progressiven italienischen Designtheorie. Sie machten Probleme der Stadtplanung zum Ausgangspunkt ausgiebiger philosophischer Diskussionen und untersuchten, wie der Mitbegründer und Sprecher von Archizoom, Andrea Branzi, es formulierte, »die neue Pop-Szene«, ohne dabei die »Architektur als politisches Instrument« auszuschließen. Der Architekt hatte die Stellung und die Verantwortung eines Schamanen in einer Gesellschaft mit komplexen sprituellen und emotionalen, materiellen und praktischen Bedürfnissen erlangt.

un langage de tous les jours, quelque chose à mettre à côté des engins spatiaux, des ordinateurs et des produits jetables d'une ère électro-atomique.»

L'Exposition de 1967, à Montréal, offrit aux créateurs un contexte dans lequel les architectes pouvaient explorer ces possibilités nouvelles, en utilisant les technologies industrielles de pointe pour créer des structures théâtrales et symboliques. Le dôme géodésique de Buckminster Fuller, «Habitat», le projet d'habitation modulaire de Moshe Safdie et le pavillon allemand en forme de tente de Rolf Gutbrod et Frei Otto, avec ses poteaux, ses filets métalliques et sa membrane de plastique, représentent cet effort pour mettre au point un langage architectural expressif approprié.

Dans son essai «Complexity and Contradiction in Architecture» (1966), Venturi a touché au problème crucial du symbolisme et de la métaphore. Au même moment, deux agences de design et d'architecture, Archizoom et Superstudio, toutes deux fondées en 1966 dans un contexte de rébellion étudiante à la faculté d'architecture de Florence, lançaient un défi au modernisme institutionnalisé. Elles insistaient sur ces complexités et ces contradictions inhérentes à l'architecture qui, disaient-elles, ne pouvaient se faire dans l'isolement. Elles devinrent le vivier du design théorique italien. Pour ces créateurs, pas de discussion hors d'une réflexion sur l'urbanisme ni, pour citer le fondateur et porte-parole d'Archizoom, Andrea Branzi, sans l'étude préalable «de la scène pop». Ce qui n'excluait pas «l'architecture comme outil politique». L'architecte se voyait investi d'un rôle de gourou dans une société dont les besoins spririrituels, émotionnels et matériels étaient complexes.

Project for Fulham overlaid on aerial photograph of the district, published as the cover to "Architecture: city sense" by Theo Crosby, who stated in the text that "The new city must arise out of the old as an extension of its spirit", 1965

"Helix City" model by **Kisho Kurokawa**, 1961

"Helix City" project by **Kisho Kurokawa**, 1961

"Habitat" modular dwelling system, designed by **Moshe Safdie**, built for Expo '67, Montreal

Axonometric illustration of **Moshe Safdie**'s "Habitat" design

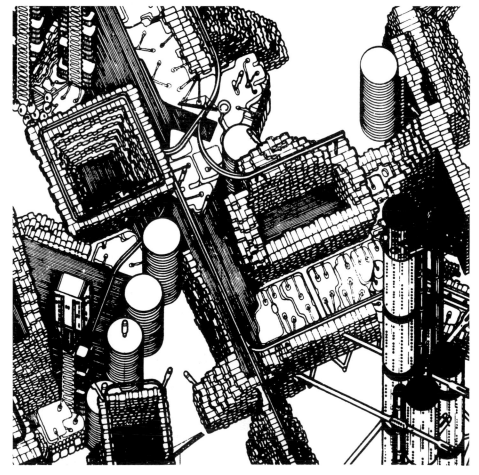

TOP AND RIGHT
Geodesic Dome, designed
by **Buckminster Fuller**
for Expo '67, Montreal

Project for a city transit corridor in the sky, designed by **Barna von Satory** and **Georg Kohlmaier**, 1969

The Post Office Tower, London, designed by **G. R. Yeats**, 1965

PAGE **136** TOP
The German pavilion at Expo '67, a tent-like structure in steel and nylon, designed by **Frei Otto** and **Rolf Gutbrod**, 1967

PAGE **136** BOTTOM AND **137**
Olympic stadium in Tokyo, designed by **Kenzo Tange**, 1964

ZOOM....INTO A POP-UP WORLD OF TOWERS....PROTOTYPES OF THE CITY OF THE FUTURE ....
RINGED BY THE CITY OF ZOOM....HERE ARE FOUR PROJECTS FOR TOWERS FOR AN INTERNATIONAL
EXHIBITION....tower(1) is by Warren Chalk, every level revolves, the bubbles which
make up the tower shine and are constantly different....the completely chameleonic building.

tower(2) by Ron Herron is
a complex of tubes, bulging
and grasping light, a play
city in the vertical......

in tower(3) by Frank Linden, the shafts rise clear and metallic above
and through the plugged-in entertainments rooms, the cage is diagonal
the communication ties are horizontal......
tower(4) by Peter Cook spreads a net of structure and drapes a skin
around the tower, the outcrop occurs again at the middle and top of
the structure, movement is always on the diagonal......

"Prototype of the city of the
future – Towers for an International Exhibition", incorporating projects by Warren Chalk,
Peter Cook, Ron Herron and
Frank Linden, from "Archigram", issue 4, 1964

"Archigram", issue 4, 1964

"Wind City", architectural project by **Archizoom**, 1969

"Project for Manhattan" by **Superstudio**, from the film "Il Monumento continuo", 1969

TOP AND LEFT
Project model for a tower of
dwellings in prefabricated
cylinders, designed by **Guy
Dessauges**, c. 1966

TOP AND BOTTOM
The first full plastic house,
designed by **Dieter Schmid**,
1965

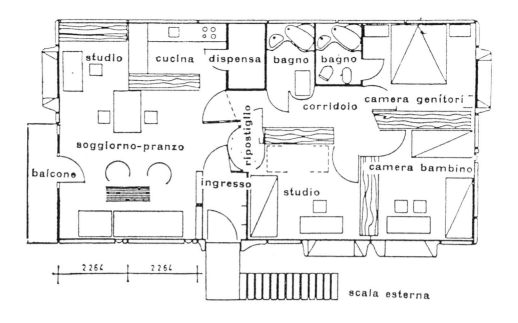

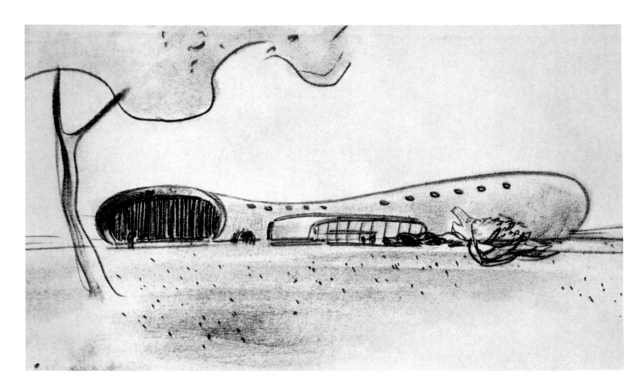

TOP AND PAGE **143**
Drawing and model of a
tunnel for aerodynamic
experiments with cars,
designed by **Angelo
Mangiarotti**, 1965

Urban sign systems, Tokyo, 1962

Signs in a booklet cover design for I. C. I. by **Fletcher**, **Forbes** and **Gill**, c. 1966

Urban sign systems, Berlin,
1965

The Frankfurt ring road and
motorway intersection, built
1962–65

Neon sign for the Stardust
Hotel and Casino, Las Vegas,
designed by **Paul Miller** for
Ad-Art, 1965

Neon sign for the Flamingo
Hotel and Casino, Las Vegas,
1967

PAGE **147**
Sign for the Horseshoe
casino, Las Vegas, designed
by **Wayne McAllister** and
William Wagner, 1962

In architecture as in most areas of design through the 20th century, the Modern Movement has cast a long shadow. Modernism has been the most tenacious influence, widely perceived as the absolute goal, the defining standard of theory and form. The disciples of Modernism, from vociferous early exponents such as Viennese architect Adolf Loos, who claimed "ornament is crime", to chroniclers such as historian Nikolaus Pevsner, author of the seminal 1936 study *Pioneers of the Modern Movement* (revised and retitled *Pioneers of Modern Design* in 1960), have suggested a linear progression of the purist ideal; so many stylistic manifestations, from Art Deco, through Surrealism to Pop styling, have been explained away by defenders of the Modernist mainstream as diversionary, indulgently decorative by-ways, very much secondary to the central issue of design.

Whilst Modernism enjoyed favour through the Sixties both as a style and as an ideology, there developed an increasingly impassioned and persuasive reaction against the advocates of purist theory and practice. Japanese architect Arata Isozaki, in his introduction to Andrea Branzi's 1984 study *The Hot House Italian New Wave Design*, recalled the challenges of the heady days of conflict and revolution. "In the mid-1960s," he wrote, "it was no longer functioning as it had in the early period of the Modern Movement … At that time, young architects from Tokyo, London, Vienna, and other centers were creating utopian technological schemes for the city of the future … But some … had already become aware that the future would not be rosy … I consider the course of modern architecture pioneered by the avant-garde to have been changed definitively and qualitatively by the confrontation resulting from the occupation of the [Milan] Triennale exhibition building in 1968, which was in turn part of a cultural revolution whose origins were in Paris."

The crisis of faith that overtook the world of design was one facet of a major socio-political upheaval which changed the mood of western society in the critical period of 1966–68. The promise of the early Sixties faded into anger, frustration and unrest. The Hippie counterculture and its allied anti-war movement in the United States, the European student revolutions of 1968 and the student occupation which closed the Milan 1968 Triennale, were symptomatic of the reappraisal of values which found its counterpart in the "Anti-Design" movement. Even the Hochschule für Gestaltung founded as a continuum of Bauhaus Modernist orthodoxy, was not immune to cultural shifts. In 1957 Max Bill had relinquished his role as director and the new board, chaired by Tomás Maldonado, led the school into a more questioning and philosophically open phase till its closure in 1968. In France the torch of anti-Establishment thinking in design was taken up by the International Situationists, led by Guy Debord,

Die Architektur wie auch die meisten anderen Gestaltungsbereiche sind im 20. Jahrhundert stark von der modernen Reformbewegung geprägt worden. Den nachhaltigsten Einfluß übte dabei der Modernismus aus, der von weiten Kreisen als absolutes Ziel, als Maßstab für Theorie und Form angesehen wurde. Die Verfechter des Modernismus – von lautstarken, frühen Vertretern wie dem Wiener Architekten Adolf Loos, der »Ornament für Verbrechen« hielt, bis zu Chronisten wie dem Historiker Nikolaus Pevsner, Autor des 1936 erschienenen Grundlagenwerks »Pioneers of the Modern Movement« (»Wegbereiter moderner Formgebung«, Köln 1983) – vertraten die Auffassung, daß sich das puristische Design konstant weiterentwickelt hätte. Das Auftreten zahlreicher anderer Stilarten wie Art déco, Surrealismus oder Pop Art taten die Befürworter des Modernismus dagegen als für das Design unerhebliche Nebenerscheinungen ab, die in bezug auf die zentrale Designproblematik von zweitrangiger Bedeutung wären.

Obwohl sich der Modernismus während der sechziger Jahre als Stil und als Ideologie immer noch großer Beliebtheit erfreute, formierte sich gleichzeitig eine immer leidenschaftlicher und überzeugender werdende Opposition, die sich gegen die Vertreter puristischer Theorien und Praktiken richtete. In seiner Einleitung zu der 1984 von Andrea Branzi heraugegebenen Studie »The Hot House Italian New Wave Design« erinnerte der japanische Architekt Arata Isozaki daran, welchen Herausforderungen man sich auf der Höhe des Konflikts und der Revolution gegenübersah: »Mitte der sechziger Jahre wurde deutlich, daß die ›Avantgarde‹ nicht mehr die Rolle spielte, wie sie das noch zu Beginn der modernen Reformbewegung getan hatte … Junge Architekten aus Tokio, London, Wien und anderen Metropolen arbeiteten zwar an utopischen technologischen Projekten für die Stadt der Zukunft … aber einigen … war bereits bewußt geworden, daß die Zukunft nicht rosig aussehen würde … Ich bin der Meinung, daß die Geschichte der modernen Architektur, die bis dahin weitgehend von der Avantgarde bestimmt wurde, durch die 1968 aus der Besetzung der Mailänder Triennale resultierende Konfrontation definitiv und qualitativ verändert worden ist. Diese Konfrontation war Bestandteil einer kulturellen Revolution, die ihren Ursprung in Paris hatte.«

Die Glaubenskrise, die über die Welt des Designs hereinbrach, war nur ein Aspekt unter den vielen soziopolitischen Veränderungen, die in der westlichen Welt während der kritischen Jahre 1966–68 zu einem Stimmungsumschwung führten. Der Traum der frühen sechziger Jahre schlug in Wut, Frustration und Unruhe um. Die Gegenkultur der Hippie-Bewegung, die mit ihr eng verbundene Anti-Kriegsbewegung in Amerika, die europäischen Studentenunruhen von 1968 sowie die Besetzung der Mailänder Triennale durch Studenten, die zur Schließung der Ausstellung führte, waren symptomatisch für den radikalen Wertewandel, der seine Ent-

En architecture comme dans la plupart des domaines
du design au 20ème siècle, le modernisme a pesé lourd
dans la balance. Il a eu une influence extrêmement
durable et a été communément considéré comme le but
à atteindre, la référence théorique et esthétique. Les
fidèles du mouvement, que ce soit l'architecte viennois
Adolf Loos, fervent apôtre de la première heure qui
proclamait que l'ornement est un crime ou des chroni-
queurs comme l'historien Nikolaus Pevsner, auteur
d'une étude publiée en 1936 et qui fit école, «Pioneers of
the Modern Movement», ont toujours fait comme si
l'idée véhiculée par le purisme se développait selon une
progression linéaire. Ces défenseurs du courant moderniste ont cherché à faire passer bien des manifestations
stylistiques, tels l'Art déco, le surréalisme, ou le style
pop pour des diversions, de petits intermèdes décoratifs, très secondaires par rapport au cœur du problème.
    Même si le style et l'idéologie modernistes ont joui
d'une grande faveur tout au long des années soixante,
un mouvement d'opposition passionnée et très persuasive réussit à se développer à l'encontre des tenants
d'une théorie et d'une pratique puristes. Dans sa préface
au livre de Andrea Branzi paru en 1984 «The Hot House
Italian New Wave Design», l'architecte japonais Arata
Isozaki rappelait cette époque tumultueuse. «Vers la
mi-décennie», écrit-il, «il apparut clairement que l'avant-
garde de l'architecture et du design ne fonctionnait plus
comme lors des débuts du Mouvement Moderne ...
C'était l'époque où de jeunes architectes à Tokyo, à
Londres, à Vienne et dans d'autres villes proposaient
des solutions alternatives à la fois utopiques et technologiques pour la cité de l'avenir ... Mais certains ...
avaient déjà compris que l'avenir ne serait pas rose ...
Je considère que, sous l'impulsion de l'avant-garde, le
cours de l'architecture moderne a été définitivement
changé le jour de l'occupation du bâtiment de l'Exposition Triennale [de Milan] en 1968 qui, à son tour, s'inscri-
vait dans une révolution culturelle qui avait commencé à
Paris.»
    La crise de conscience qui s'empara du monde du
design était une facette d'un vaste bouleversement
socio-politique qui transforma le climat de la société
occidentale en ces années critiques 1966–68. Les
espoirs des premières années de la décennie tournèrent
à la colère, à la frustration et à l'agitation. La contre-
culture hippie et le mouvement pacifiste qui s'y ratta-
chait aux Etats-Unis, la révolte étudiante de 1968 en
Europe et l'occupation par les étudiants de la Triennale
de Milan étaient symptomatiques d'une remise en
question des valeurs dont la contrepartie est le mouvement de l'«anti-design». Même l'Ecole de design d'Ulm,
qui avait été fondée pour porter le flambeau du Bauhaus
moderniste, se révéla sensible aux turbulences cultu-
relles. En 1957, Max Bill avait démissionné de son poste
de directeur et le nouveau comité de direction, présidé
par Tomás Maldonado, avait inauguré pour l'école

6

Design and Anti-Design

Design und Anti-Design

Design et anti-Design

author of such tracts as *Contre le Fonctionnalisme* and *Chaos Urbanistique*.

The "Anti-Design" movement achieved its highest profile in Italy. Ettore Sottsass played a central role in this highly charged reaction to the momentum of materialistic middle-class consumer culture. He challenged the complacency of mainstream "classic" Italian design, its success built upon bourgeois values of material quality and elegant form. "I had just started to think," he wrote in 1970 in *Domus* (No.489, p.56), "that if there was any point in designing objects, it was to be found in helping people to live somehow, I mean in helping people to somehow recognise and free themselves, I mean that if there was a point in designing objects, it could only be found in achieving a kind of therapeutic action, handing over to the objects the function of stimulating the perception of one's own adventures". Sottsass and like-minded contemporaries including the designers of the Archizoom and Superstudio groups and such notable *agents provocateurs* as Gaetano Pesce, Ugo la Pietra, the UFO group and the partnership of Lomazzi, d'Urbino and de Pas, devised thought-provoking objects, furniture and schemes. Their work challenged conventions of "good" taste, toying with kitsch, Pop and mystical metaphors.

The "Anti-Design" lobby stimulated the design scene, enlarged the repertoire, stretched horizons. Italian design was at a high point of creativity and influence. Avant-garde ideas, suitable only for exhibition or the pages of *Domus*, enriched the language of commercial design and gave Italian products a unique layering of reference, even in works which at first glance suggest an allegiance to purist principles. Gae Aulenti, Mario Bellini, Achille Castiglioni, Joe Colombo, Enzo Mari, Richard Sapper, Tobia Scarpa and Marco Zanuso were amongst the most talented of the roll-call of designers to give classic, beautiful, yet personal form to manufactured products through this period.

The craft revival of the Sixties defined an alternative reaction to the depersonalisation of the design and manufacturing processes. The self-conscious rekindling of the values of creative artisanship generated a significant following, notably in the fields of studio ceramics and glass. Potters Hans Coper, Lucie Rie, Peter Voulkos and Ruth Duckworth were amongst the most gifted exponents of their medium; in the United States, Dominic Labino and Harvey Littleton founded the studio glass movement and created artifacts which questioned the divide between the fine and applied arts. The cherishing of craft traditions was always central to Scandinavian culture and was fully expressed in the Sixties in an variety of media, from hand-wrought silverware to glass sculpture or the "rya" woven rugs which provide a focal point to so many Scandinavian

sprechung in der »Anti-Design«-Bewegung fand. Selbst die Nachfolgeinstitution des orthodox-modernistischen Bauhauses, die Hochschule für Gestaltung in Ulm, war nicht immun gegen kulturelle Strömungen. Bereits 1957 war Max Bill von seinem Posten als Direktor der Hochschule zurückgetreten. Das neue Direktorium unter dem Vorsitz von Tomás Maldonado führte die Schule in eine kritischere und philosophisch aufgeschlossene Phase bis zu ihrer Schließung im Jahr 1968. In Frankreich formulierten die Internationalen Situationisten unter der Führung von Guy Debord, dem Autor von Abhandlungen wie »Contre le Fonctionnalisme« und »Chaos Urbanistique«, die Kritik am etablierten modernistischen Design.

Die »Anti-Design«-Bewegung erfuhr ihre stärkste Ausprägung in Italien. Ettore Sottsass war ein besonders bekannter Vertreter derer, die so heftig auf die absolut materialistische Konsumkultur der Mittelklasse reagierten. Er forderte die Eitelkeit des dominierenden »klassischen« italienischen Designs, dessen Erfolg auf bürgerlichen Werten wie Materialqualität und eleganter Formgebung beruhte, heraus. 1970 formulierte er in der Zeitschrift »Domus« (Nr. 489, S.56): »Ich bin zu der Überzeugung gekommen, daß, wenn es überhaupt einen Sinn macht, Gegenstände zu entwerfen, er nur darin liegen kann, den Menschen das Leben irgendwie zu erleichtern und es ihnen zu ermöglichen, sich selbst zu erkennen und zu befreien; ich meine, wenn das Entwerfen von Gegenständen einen Sinn machen soll, kann dieser nur darin bestehen, eine Art therapeutischer Wirkung zu erzielen, indem man den Gegenständen neben ihrer Funktion auch die Aufgabe überträgt, das Wahrnehmungsvermögen des Betrachters zu reizen.« Sottsass und gleichgesinnte Zeitgenossen, darunter die Designer der Gruppen Archizoom und Superstudio und so bekannte »agents provocateurs« wie Gaetano Pece, Ugo la Pietra, die Gruppe UFO und das Trio Lomazzi, d'Urbino und de Pas entwarfen Objekte, Möbel und Systeme, die den Intellekt provozierten. Ihre Arbeiten, die vom spielerischen Umgang mit Kitsch, Pop und mystischen Metaphern zeugten, forderten die Konventionen des »guten« Designs heraus.

Die »Anti-Design«-Lobby stimulierte die Designszene, sie vergrößerte das Repertoire und erweiterte Horizonte. Das italienische Design befand sich in einem kreativen Hoch und übte international einen enormen Einfluß aus. Extravagante, avantgardistische Ideen, die eigentlich nur für Ausstellungen oder für die Veröffentlichung in der Zeitschrift »Domus« geeignet waren, bereicherten die kommerzielle Designsprache und führten dazu, daß den italienischen Produkten eine einzigartige stilistische Vorreiterrolle zukam. Dieser Umstand betraf sogar Objekte, die auf den ersten Blick eine gewisse Loyalität gegenüber puristischen Prinzipien erkennen ließen. Gae Aulenti, Mario Bellini, Achille Castiglioni, Joe Colombo, Enzo Mari, Richard Sapper, Tobia Scarpa und Marco

jusqu'à sa fermeture en 1968 une phase moins dogmatique, plus ouverte sur la réflexion. En France, ce furent les Situationnistes Internationaux qui défendirent la cause des non-conformistes du design. Leur chef était Guy Debord, auteur de pamphlets comme «Contre le fonctionnalisme» et «Chaos urbanistique».

C'est en Italie que l'«anti-design» se montra sous son jour le plus intéressant. Ettore Sottsass joua un rôle primordial dans cette forte réaction face à la très vigoureuse culture matérialiste de la bourgeoisie. Il dénonça la complaisance du courant «classique» du design italien, qui s'était construit sur les valeurs bourgeoises de qualité et d'esthétisme. «Je commençais à penser», écrit-il en 1970 dans le magazine «Domus» (No. 489, p. 56),» que si créer des objets avait un sens, c'était d'une certaine façon d'aider les gens à vivre. Je veux dire, de les aider à faire des constatations et à devenir plus libres. Ce que je veux dire, c'est que si le design a un sens, ce ne peut être que celui, thérapeutique, de conférer aux objets une fonction stimulatrice, de faire qu'ils nous aident à voir dans quelle aventure nous sommes embarqués.» Sottsass et ses semblables, parmi eux les designers d'Archizoom et de Superstudio ainsi que de notables «agents provocateurs» comme Gaetano Pesce, Ugo la Pietra, le groupe UFO et les créateurs associés Lomazzi, d'Urbino et de Pas, produisirent des objets, des meubles et des projets originaux. Leurs travaux remettaient en question les conventions du «bon» goût et flirtaient avec le kitsch, le style pop et la métaphore mystique.

Le lobby «anti-design» fut une stimulation pour toute la discipline, il en élargit le répertoire et les horizons. Le design italien était alors très créatif, très influent. Ces idées d'avant-garde, qui n'étaient guère destinées qu'aux pages de «Domus», enrichirent néanmoins le langage du design commercial et permirent aux créations italiennes d'atteindre une densité inédite, même dans des œuvres qui, au premier coup d'œil, semblent répondre aux critères puristes. Gae Aulenti, Mario Bellini, Achille Castiglioni, Joe Colombo, Enzo Mari, Richard Sapper, Tobia Scarpa et Macro Zanuso sont autant de créateurs doués qui ont marqué la production de l'époque du sceau d'un style classique, esthétique mais aussi très personnel.

La renaissance de l'artisanat dans les années soixante contribua à créer un courant de réaction contre la dépersonnalisation du design et des processus de fabrication. Les conséquences de cet effort pour remettre en vigueur la créativité artisanale se firent notamment sentir dans les domaines de la céramique et de la verrerie d'art. Les potiers Hans Coper, Lucie Rie, Peter Voulkos et Ruth Duckworth sont à citer parmi les représentants les plus doués de leur spécialité. Aux Etats-Unis, Dominic Labino et Harvey Littleton fondèrent un nouveau mouvement de verriers d'art et créèrent des pièces qui permettent de douter qu'une barrière sépare beaux-arts et arts appli-

Demonstration at the Triennale, Milan, 1968

interiors. The crafts allowed a synthesis of the processes of conception and creation; they became a celebration of the heart, the eye and the hand working in unison. Craft creativity could be at once intimate and transcendental.

The Anti-Design movement and the craft revival recast the very idea of design, proposing a far more personal quality of gesture, a celebration of the human spirit and imagination. The social and political implications were evident. In 1967 thirty-five thousand peace protestors marched to the steps of the Pentagon to be met by a wall of raised rifles. A protestor stepped from the crowd and started to place pink carnations in the barrels. His gesture captured the spirit of a generation seeking to design a better future.

Zanuso gehörten zu den großen Könnern, die den Industrieprodukten dieser Zeit einen klassischen, schönen, aber auch persönlichen Ausdruck verliehen.

Als Reaktion auf die immer unpersönlicheren Gestaltungs- und Produktionsverfahren erlebte das Kunsthandwerk in den sechziger Jahren eine Renaissance. Selbstbewußt propagierte man die wiederentdeckten Werte einer kreativen Handwerkskunst und mobilisierte damit, insbesondere in den Bereichen Studio-Keramik und Studio-Glas, eine beachtliche Gefolgschaft. Keramiker wie Hans Coper, Lucie Rie, Peter Voulkos und Ruth Duckworth gehörten zu den begabtesten Vertretern ihres Faches. In Amerika begründeten Dominic Labino und Harvey Littleton die Studio-Glas-Bewegung und schufen Kunstwerke, die die Grenzen zwischen den freien und den angewandten Künsten in Frage stellten. Für die skandinavische Kultur war die Erhaltung handwerklicher Traditionen schon immer von zentraler Bedeutung. In den sechziger Jahren konnte man das an verschiedenen kunstgewerblichen Objekten wie den handgeschmiedeten Silberwaren, den Glasskulpturen oder den »Rya«-Teppichen, die den Blickfang so vieler skandinavischer Einrichtungen bildeten, deutlich ablesen. Das Kunsthandwerk ermöglichte die Synthese von Entwurfs- und Fertigungsprozessen, es ermöglichte das einvernehmliche Zusammenwirken von Herz, Auge und Hand und führte so zu schöpferischen Glanzpunkten. Kunsthandwerkliche Kreativität konnte gleichzeitig intim und raumübergreifend sein.

Die »Anti-Design«-Bewegung und die Renaissance des Kunsthandwerks führten zu einer Neuformulierung der Designidee. Sie bewirkten eine sehr viel eigenständigere Qualität des individuellen Ausdrucks und erbrachten Höchstleistungen im Bereich des menschlichen Geistes und seiner Vorstellungskraft. Die sozialen und politischen Implikationen lagen auf der Hand. 1967 zogen 35000 Friedensdemonstranten vor die Stufen des Pentagons, wo sie auf eine Phalanx von angelegten Gewehren stießen. Ein Demonstrant löste sich aus der Menge und steckte rote Nelken in die Gewehrläufe. Diese Geste war charakteristisch für den Geist einer Generation, die auf der Suche nach einer besseren Zukunft war.

qués. La culture scandinave avait toujours donné une place de choix à l'artisanat et, dans les années soixante, celui-ci s'exprima en de nombreux médias, depuis le travail de l'argent jusqu'aux sculptures de verre et aux tapis tissés à la main «rya», qui sont le point de mire de tant d'intérieurs scandinaves. L'artisanat permettait la synthèse des processus de conception et de création en une célébration pour laquelle le cœur, l'œil et la main travaillaient à l'unison. La créativité artisanale pouvait être à la fois intime et transcendantale.

Le mouvement anti-design et la renaissance de l'artisanat placèrent dans une lumière nouvelle l'idée même de design, rendant possible une qualité bien plus humaine du geste, une fête de l'imagination et de l'esprit. Les implications sociales et politiques en étaient évidentes. En 1967, trente-cinq mille personnes participèrent à une marche pour la paix jusqu'aux marches du Pentagone où des fusils furent pointés sur elles. L'une d'elles sortit de la foule et mit des œillets roses dans les canons. Ce geste contient tout l'esprit d'une génération désireuse de créer un avenir meilleur.

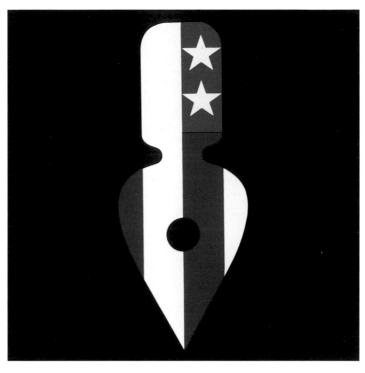

Logo for Graphics Arts USA, designed by **Tom Geismar** of Chermayeff & Geismar Inc, 1963

Scene from the film "Easy Rider", 1969

TOP RIGHT
Armchair, designed by **Gunnar Andersen**, 1964–65

LEFT
Manufacturing Andersen's armchair at the Dansk Poly- ther Industri, Frederiksund, Denmark, c. 1964–65

"Pave Piuma" floor elements, designed by **Piero Gilardi**, 1965

"Pratone", prototype seat, designed by **Giorgio Ceretti, Piero Derossi** and **Ricardo Rosso** for Gufram, polyurethane, 1966

"Bulb" lamps, designed by
Ingo Maurer, 1968

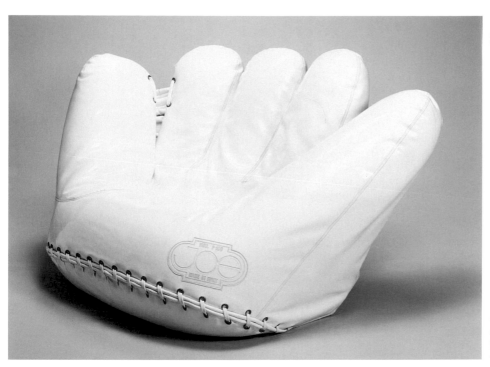

"Joe" chair, designed by
Jonathan De Pas, homage to
the baseball champion Joe Di
Maggio, 1970

"Pillola" lamps, designed by
Cesare Casati and **Emanuele
Ponzio**, 1968, produced from
1969 by Ponteur

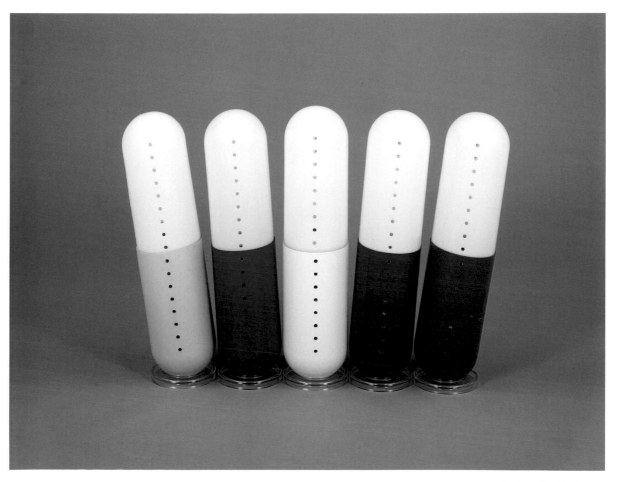

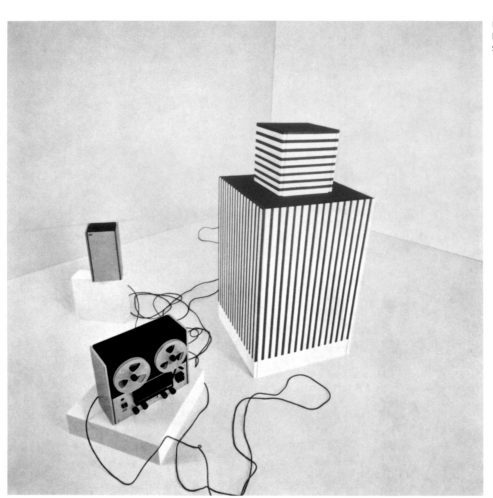

Poltronova cabinet in striped laminate, designed by **Ettore Sottsass Jr.**, 1966

Poltronova "Asteroide" lamp, designed by **Ettore Sottsass Jr.**, 1968

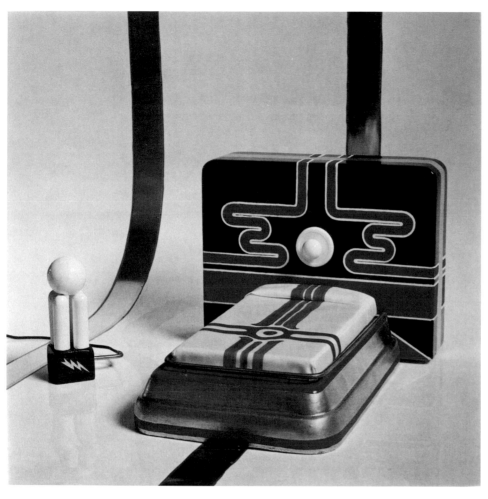

"Elettro Rosa" bed, from the series "Rosa Imperiale", and "Atlante" lamp, designed by **Archizoom**, 1967

Poltronova "Mies" chair, designed by **Archizoom**, 1969

Six phases of pumping up the "Up" chair

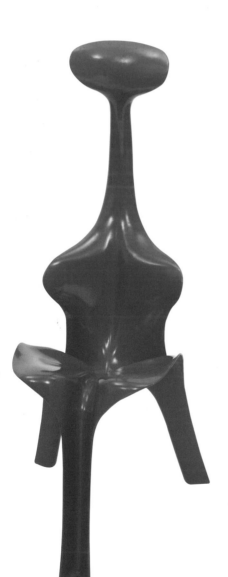

Advertisement for "Up" chairs, designed by **Gaetano Pesce**, 1969

Anthropomorphic "Floris" chair, designed by **Günter Beltzig**, fibreglass, 1963

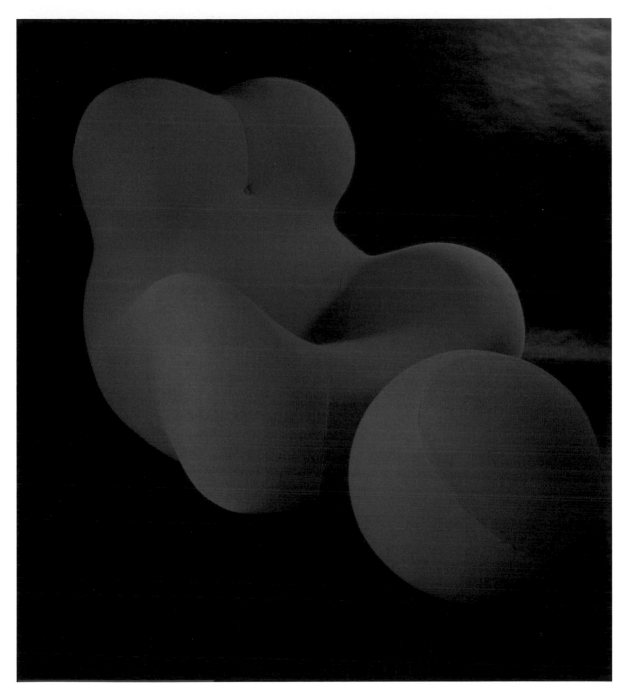

"Up 5" chair, designed by
Gaetano Pesce, 1969

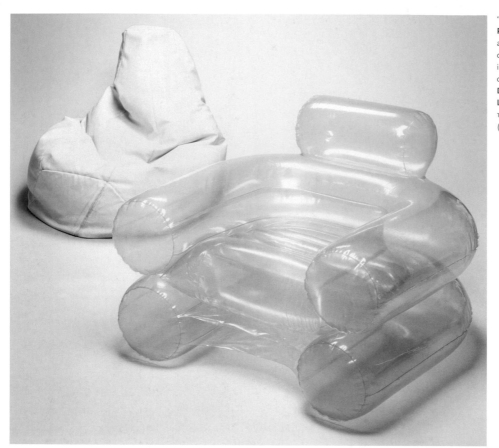

"Sacco" chair, designed by **Piero Gatti, Cesare Paolini** and **Franco Téodoro**, 1968, produced by Zanotta (left) and inflatable "Blow" armchair, designed by **Jonathan De Pas, Donato D'Urbino, Paolo Lomazzi** and **Carla Scolari**, 1967, produced by Zanotta (right)

Pneumatic apartment (6 m diameter) with inflatable walls, chairs and lamps, designed by **Quasar Khanh**, 1968

PAGE **163**
Showroom of Zanotta di Lissone, designed by **Jonathan De Pas, Donato D'Urbino** and **Paolo Lomazzi**, 1968

TOP AND BOTTOM
Cardboard child's chair,
designed by **Peter Murdoch**,
1963, produced 1964–65 by
International Paper

Eye and Bob Dylan motifs on
on dresses by **Poster Dresses**,
1967

"Tube-chair", designed by **Joe
Colombo**, plastic and foam,
1969

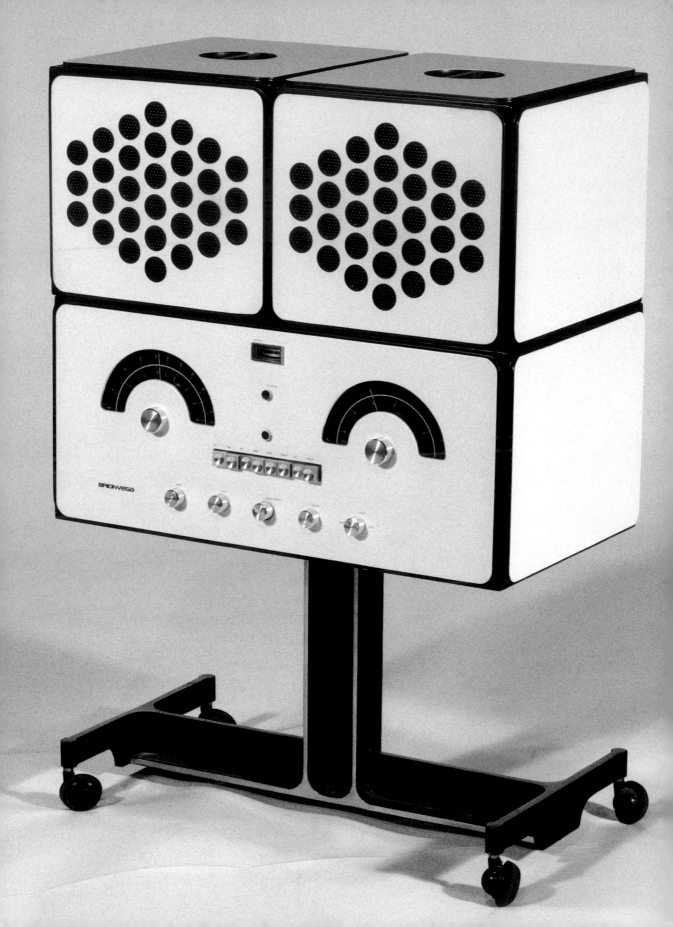

TOP LEFT
Carrying case for Brionvega
"Black 12" television, plastic,
1969

TOP RIGHT
Brionvega "Black 12" television, designed by **Richard
Sapper** and **Marco Zanuso**,
1969

"Clam" ashtray, designed by
Pentagram, late 1960s

PAGE **166**
Brionvega record player,
designed by **Achille and Pier
Giacomo Castiglioni**, 1966

Sirrah "MT" lamp, designed
by **Giancarlo Mattiolo**, metal,
1969

Kartell floor ashtray, designed
by **Joe Colombo**, metal and
plastic, 1968–70

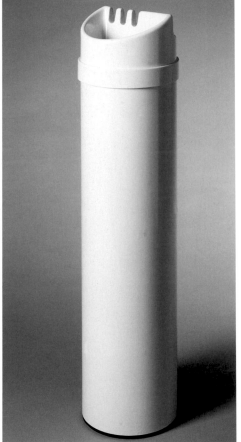

Riz-Italora "Optic" clock,
designed by **Joe Colombo**,
c. 1970

PAGE **169**
"Pipistrello" lamp, designed
by **Gae Aulenti**, metal base,
plastic shade, 1965, manufactured by Martinelli Luce
from 1966

Danese "Pago-Pago" vase,
designed by **Enzo Mari**,
plastic, 1969

PAGE **171**
Stacking chairs, designed by
Joe Colombo, nylon and
polypropylene, 1965, manufactured by Kartell from 1967

BOTTOM
Olivetti "Valentine" typewriter,
designed by **Ettore Sottsass Jr.**
and **Perry King**, 1969

"Apple tree" rya rug by **Norma Heimola**

Free-form glass vase by **Sam Herman**, 1965

Ash-glazed stoneware vase by
Ruth Duckworth, c. 1967

Ceramic vase, designed by
Hans Coper, its form
described by the potter as
"like Saturn with its rings",
c. 1966

Stoneware dish, designed by
Lucie Rie, c. 1965

"Peace" poster, designed by **Robert Brownjohn** shortly before his death in 1970

Graphic motif of a head literally bursting with visual ideas, designed by **Riccardo Manzi** for Pirelli to illustrate in a corporate publication a feature on the future of graphic design, 1965

PAGE 175
Advertisement by the French firm "Print", 1968

ARE YOU ONE TOO?

=

PEACE

TAKE IT OR LEAVE IT

GO NAKED

CREAZ. DIXY-BOY

=

STAMP OUT REALITY

MAKE LOVE NOT WAR

SUPPORT YOUR LOCAL BUTTON MERCHANT

9 OUT OF 10 OLD MAIDS PREFER The New York Times

blam! POW
hud
oof! sock!
CREAZ. DIXY-BOY

BATMAN & ROBIN

STAMP OUT PAY TOILETS

DRAFT BEER NOT STUDENTS

A A

YOU INTEREST ME

Peace News

MAKE LOVE NOT WAR

SOCRATES EATS HEMLOCK

chitarre contro la guerra

sono un mostro
venuto dallo spazio

100

SAVE WATER SHOWER WITH A FRIEND

non vogliamo morire per voi

WE SHALL OVERCOME

Y POPPINS IS A JUNKIE

PEANUT BUTTER IS BETTER THAN POT

STUDENT POWER

Acknowledgements

The author wishes to express his thanks to the many people who have helped in the research and preparation of this book, including Peter Cook (Archigram), Ann Creed, Anne-Marie Ehrlich, Richard Fahey (Chermayeff & Geismar), Robin Farrow, Karen Fielder (Sainsbury's PLC), Martin Harrison, Helen Mapes (Hille International Ltd), David A. Mellor, Heather Naylor (Knoll International Ltd), Richard Rutledge (Herman Miller Inc.) and Winston Spriet. He is particularly grateful to Clarissa Bruce for the very high quality of the many photographs taken by her specially for this project. Angelika Muthesius has been an enthusiastic and sympathetic editor and her input in the picture research proved particularly valuable. Many of the illustrations are from the author's archive. The credits on this page provide specific acknowledgement of artist and other copyrights. Last but by no means least the author wishes to thank his family, Lucilla and Dominic, and colleagues, Siobhan Anderson and Lydia Cresswell-Jones, for their constant support.

The publisher wishes to thank Erich Wagner from the Deutsches Architekturmuseum, Frankfurt, and Uwe Dettmar, Frankfurt, for their support.

Credits
(t = top, b = bottom, l = left, r = right)
Despite intensive research it has not always been possible to establish copyright ownership. Where this is the case we would appreciate notification.

2/3 © National Screen Service Ltd.
6/7 Museum Ludwig, Cologne/ Photo: Rheinisches Bildarchiv, Cologne
11 b Photo: Richard Bryant/Arcaid
15 Photo: Courtesy NASA, Life Magazine © Time Inc.
17 Polygram Int. Ltd., London
20/21 Courtesy of Knoll Archives, New York
28/29 Courtesy of Knoll Archives, New York
32 t Herman Miller Archives
36 b Torsten Bröhan, Düsseldorf
38/39 Institut für Baugeschichte, University of Karlsruhe/Photo: Horstheinz Neuendorff, Baden-Baden
42 b Kunstgewerbemuseum, Berlin/ Photo: Saturia Linke, Berlin
43 © Verner Panton, Basle
44 Stelton, Denmark/Photo: E. Christiansen
46 bl OLuce, Milano
51 Herman Miller Archives/ Photo: Baltazar Kareg
57 Museum Ludwig, Cologne/ Photo: Rheinisches Bildarchiv, Cologne

59 © Allen Jones, London
60 © Robert Indiana
61 © Robert Indiana
64 © William Klein, Paris/Focus, Hamburg
66t © United Press International (UK) Ltd. London
74l © Vogue, The Condé Nast Publications Ltd., London
75t © William Klein, Paris/Focus, Hamburg
76t © Bridget Riley, London
89 © National Screen Service Ltd.
91 © Verner Panton, Basle
93b © Verner Panton, Basle
99 © Courrèges Design, Paris
101 © 1968 Turner Entertainment Co., All Rights Reserved
102t Photo: Jürgens Ost und Europa Photo, Berlin
103 © USIS, Bonn
105 Photo: Ed Pfizenmaier
108t Courtesy of Knoll Archives, New York
110t + b © Fondation pour l'Architecture/ L'Utopie du Tout Plastique 1960–1973
112b © Fondation pour l'Architecture/ L'Utopie du Tout Plastique 1960–1973
114b © Verner Panton, Basle
115 Photo: Bayer AG, Leverkusen
116t © Warner Fabrics plc
116b Photo: Vitra Design Museum, Weil am Rhein
118t + b, © 1968 Turner Entertainment Co.,
119t All Rights Reserved
119b Courtesy Fischer Fine Art Ltd., London
120t Kunstgewerbemuseum, Berlin/ Photo: Saturia Linke, Berlin
124b © Fondation pour l'Architecture/ L'Utopie du Tout Plastique 1960–1973
132t Photo: Tomio Ohashi
133t Photo: The Architectural Press
135b Photo: Zefa Picture Library (UK) Ltd.
136/137 Photo: The Architectural Press
138t + b © Archigram Archives, London
144t, 145t Photo: Popperfoto, Northampton
145b © Hans Schmied/ZEFA, Düsseldorf
153b Columbia Pictures
154l Skala-magazine for architecture and art; Grete Aagaard Andersen, Hellebæk/Photos: Schnakenburg & Brahl fotografi, Copenhagen
154t Courtesy of Musée des Arts décoratifs de Montréal, The Liliane & David M. Stewart Collection/Photo: Richard P. Goodbody, New York
157t © Fondation pour l'Architecture/ L'Utopie du Tout Plastique 1960–1973
162t © Fondation pour l'Architecture/ L'Utopie du Tout Plastique 1960–1973
165b © Fondation pour l'Architecture/ L'Utopie du Tout Plastique 1960–1973